DETHRONING

your

INNER CRITIC

DETHRONING

your

INNER CRITIC

The Four-Step Journey from
Self-Doubt to Self-Empowerment

Joanna Kleinman, LCSW

ADVANCE PRAISE

"THE #1 MUST-READ BOOK OF THE CENTURY FOR WOMEN! Whether you're struggling with a crisis or a challenge, or you need to safeguard yourself against haters or habitual inner critic BS, this book will help you kiss pessimism and pandemonium good-bye so you can finally be the queen of the castle in your own life! #EnoughSaid?!"

—Janine Driver, New York Times best-selling author of *You Say More Than You Think*

"Joanna Kleinman has translated her deep well of experience as a psychotherapist into this helpful and supportive guide to self-love. Far from a distant and unreachable guru, Joanna's willingness to share her own journey allows us to trust her guidance and wisdom. Her M.I.N.D. process will help readers notice and disrupt their Inner Critic and come home to their Authentic Self."

—Alexandra H. Solomon, PhD, licensed clinical psychologist and best-selling author of *Loving Bravely* and *Taking Sexy Back*

"An engaging exploration of the dialogue so many women have running through our heads. Joanna Kleinman offers a clear-cut, step-by-step method to shift out of your automatic negative programming and into a whole new way of thinking. The ability to shift the lens is transformative."

—Lois Nachamie, author of *So Glad We Waited: A Hand-Holding Guide for Over-35 Parents* (foreword by Debra Winger) and *Big Lessons for Little People: Teaching Our Kids Right from Wrong While Keeping Them Healthy, Safe and Happy*

"We all have that inner idiot who causes self-sabotage and who wants us to live in fear. It can be overwhelming. Joanna has pioneered a method to help you recognize that inner idiot, then exorcise it from your mind, so that you can become who you were really meant to be: a whole, complete, fully expressed, powerful soul. If you're ready to finally break free, this book will give you step-by-step guidance on how to do just that."

—Rebecca Zung, best-selling author of
Negotiate Like You M.A.T.T.E.R.

To my husband Jon, who is my rock,
and my kids Max, Zach, and Amanda,
who are my greatest joy and provide me
with endless opportunities to practice
Dethroning my Inner Critic

CONTENTS

FOREWORD

Though this book is being published at the height of a pandemic, it's no coincidence that over the last few years, women have been in the throes of a different kind of epidemic – the epidemic of listening to *that voice*. The one that keeps us stuck in our fears. The one that wreaks havoc on our sense of peace and balance. The one that cements us in our negative thoughts. And so begins a vicious cycle that causes our lives to, well, suck.

Admitting your "stuckness" is the first step toward wiggling your way out of this quicksand you actually allowed your mind to walk you right into.

When others hurt us, we're quick to forgive. But when we inflict pain on ourselves, we opt for the harshest punishment. Instead of firing that negative voice in our heads, the one Joanna calls our Inner Critic, we freaking *promote* it. And give it a raise.

WTF?

That is why you have to read this book.

It can help you rethink how you see yourself in a way you were never, ever taught to think. It can help you erase the BS *you* trained yourself to respond to. It can help you override the self-doubt and second-guessing and fear and "what if" thinking.

In a way, you taught your mind to hurt you. In another way, it's not your fault. The flaw in your thinking was blatantly passed down from those who came before you, delivered in a package you didn't even recognize about who you're supposed to be. Comparing yourself to an idealized version of a woman who doesn't exist.

We're all guilty, in one way or another.

When I met Joanna Kleinman in 2014, she introduced me to Rita. Rita is my Inner Critic, a familiar stranger who I didn't even realize I had long ago invited to take up real estate in my head.

I was a single mom of two fabulous grown women, and had left a celebrated, 34-year career as a TV producer with NBC News and Warner Brothers to build my dream I call Campowerment.

Campowerment is a transformational playground for women to learn, connect, grow, and take a quantum leap forward. Infused with friendship, life's grounding lessons, and the spirit of the campfire, Campowerment is an incubator for agents of change who, together, become unstoppable, guided by dozens and dozens of thought leaders and authors and game-changers I met in my three decades of storytelling on TV.

Oprah wrote about Campowerment and blew up our business. We were quickly building a community of women looking to uplevel their lives through the power of playtime.

The day I met Joanna, she had read about what we do and was hungry to hear more. She invited me to share my pride over the thousands of women who had re-ignited their lives at Campowerment, but I talked more about the challenges of running a start-up business. I told her that I wasn't a great businessperson and had to sell my house to keep the lanterns on.

She was horrified. She had been so impressed by what we had built, she expected me to sing its praises. Instead, I beat myself up for what *wasn't* working. That's when Joanna introduced me to Rita, who kept beating me up for not celebrating my wins and being so crazy hard on myself.

So of course I invited Joanna to come be an expert at Campowerment in January of 2015.

In her one-hour workshop, I learned how to unhook from Rita. To literally rewire my mind to create brand new emotions that could have me taking new actions, to help me create an entirely different life than the one I had been living. Joanna basically taught me how to tell Rita to shut up and move outta my way.

How?

Imagine you have an on or off switch for your mind. That you could recognize the difference between you and the voice of your Inner Critic, and at any time, *switch off* your automatic mind and *shift into* a new mindset with entirely new thoughts.

When you start to think in a way that gets you in touch with who you really are, in ways that you love, and recognize what you already have in your life that you're grateful for, you can silence your Inner Critic. When you pivot and shift into what you already *love* about your life, you will see that nothing was ever really broken in the first place.

And that will take you to radical self-acceptance, to come from a brand new place of loving and being at peace with yourself so you can start to make new choices that bring joy and peace into your life.

Over the past five years, Joanna has been a regular fixture at Campowerment, and hundreds in our community have had their lives transformed by her process – both at camp and in her programs that followed. And now, she's become one of the Founding Members of this virtual community we call Campowerment. Because her program is epic.

See, it all starts with how we think. While you can't change your thoughts, you must first understand that you are *not* them. From Joanna, you will learn that who you are is entirely separate from your thoughts.

The concept is simple, but its impact is profound.

Most days, I don't even listen to Rita anymore. My wish for you is that you learn how to stop listening to *your* Rita too. This book can teach you how.

From the campfire and beyond,
Tammi Leader Fuller
Founder/Chief Vision Officer, Campowerment

INTRODUCTION

There's a little voice inside you with an outsized degree of influence over everything you think, say, and do. I call this voice your Inner Critic (IC), and she's the Queen of Mean.

From the time you were a child, your IC has been nattering at you, narrating your day and criticizing your every move. She's always there, but she's been so integrated into your thoughts and your reality that you don't see her as separate from you. Sometimes you just feel bad, and you're not even sure why.

We each live with our own personal version of this voice, this Inner Critic who is harsh and critical. We've been conditioned to listen to her since childhood, when we first climbed aboard a hamster wheel of striving to keep up with her demands. And we continue trying to measure up to her standards and ideals – even when they can't realistically be met.

We are vulnerable to the IC because most of us were never taught how to think. Instead of learning to practice mental discernment, we simply follow our minds along a well-worn path to the same negative thoughts, the same distorted vision of what our Inner Critic believes life to be. As a result, we focus not on what works but on what we think we can fix, change, or perfect. Only then, we believe, can we be happy.

It's a trap, and it can feel like an inescapable one. But there's an out. Once we see the difference between the Inner Critic and us, once we hear her lies for what they are, we can free ourselves from her clutches and criticism and live a more peaceful and satisfying life. This ongoing commitment to curiosity and discovery is what I call Dethroning Your Inner Critic (DYIC).

DYIC is the articulation of a process I originally created for myself alone. I follow this practice every day to rewire the way I think, and it has changed the trajectory of my life. I've also had the profound privilege of helping thousands of other people create

iv

meaningful breakthroughs in their lives through DYIC. This is powerful stuff.

In over twenty-five years as a psychotherapist, I've found that while most people say they just want to be happy, they also find happiness elusive, something over the next hill or around the bend. They believe that if they can simply be more, achieve more, fix this, or toggle that, they will be free.

You may believe this too. But I want to teach you a new way to think.

This book will show you how and why your mind – under the guise of your perpetually cranky Inner Critic – has been creating such a dissatisfactory experience of yourself and your life. You'll learn how to break free of the traps your IC sets for you and that cause your unhappiness and struggle.

You'll see the ways in which your mind has been programmed to keep you feeling stuck and alienated from the feelings you yearn for. You'll see how simple it is to get out of your own way. You'll see that Dethroning Your Inner Critic is the secret to experiencing peace, self-love, joy, personal satisfaction, and fulfillment in every area of your life. I wrote this book to help you hear her, so you can detach yourself from her.

I also wrote this book as a call to action for women in our culture. We desperately need to move away from listening to the voice of the Inner Critic within us. The voice of perfectionism, of needing to "be more disciplined," "try harder," or "have more will power." The voice that tells us we aren't good enough, smart enough, pretty enough, experienced enough.

Far too many of us allow this voice to dominate every aspect of our lives. Under the onslaught of this continual critical rant, we shrink away, keeping ourselves small in both our personal and professional lives and second-guessing our competence as mothers, partners, sisters, daughters, friends, and leaders.

The cost to women is enormous. Because we don't talk about this critical voice with each other, we don't realize we are all subject to its abuse. We project the insecurity and fear we feel inside onto others, leading us to be competitive and judgmental when instead we could be compassionate allies. The key is in all of us realizing that our Inner Critics are not, fundamentally, our true selves.

When you use the tools in this book to separate yourself from your Inner Critic, you will be able to rewire a new mind. And when you rewire a new mind, you have the opportunity to discover and listen to the real you. The Authentic Self that lies hidden within you, hidden beneath the conditioning and reflexive fear of your IC.

You don't have to dig deep into childhood wounds to figure out where your IC came from. You only need to learn how to separate yourself from the voice of your IC, and no longer give it the power to guide your thinking, your feelings, your actions, and your decisions. This book will give you the ability to quickly separate yourself from her repetitive chatter.

You can override those automatic, critical messages that keep you stuck in fear, dissatisfaction, people-pleasing, and chronic feelings of not being good enough. As women, we can rise above the negativity we feel and reclaim our power.

DETHRONING

your

INNER CRITIC

CHAPTER ONE

WHO ARE YOU REALLY?

You're a wife, a mother, a sister, a daughter, a friend. You're a teacher, or a doctor, an entrepreneur, an office worker, maybe a stay-at-home mom. You're a leader, or a high-powered executive. You may have been told that you are fun, hilarious, a good listener, and kind. You may have been told that you are aggressive, assertive, or demanding. Maybe you've been told that you are cold, selfish, controlling, and judgmental.

But consider this: What if who you think you are is only a story you've been telling yourself for your entire life – and then spent day after day, year after year, collecting evidence to prove it? By now, you have so much proof for this story you've created in your head that you can't believe there is any other version of yourself. This is simply you. Or so you think.

The truth is your sense of self, who you think you are, comes not from objective fact but rather from what you tell yourself and from what other people tell you. Your identity grows from your childhood experiences and from your ideas of what it means to be a girl, a woman, a female, or feminine. It comes from your parents and siblings, from our culture, and from your own inner sense of who you are. It comes from your thoughts. Thoughts like:

- *I'm not good enough.*
- *I can't do it.*

- *I'm not smart enough for this job. She will do it better.*
- *I'm not thin enough, or pretty enough.*
- *I can't be who they want me to be.*
- *I'm too intimidating.*
- *I'm too controlling.*

We all spend a tremendous amount of time talking and listening to that little voice in our heads. Most often the voice is admonitory and demanding – meant to constrain and prevent independent thought, much less autonomous action. Your Inner Critic voice can make you feel small, stupid, and incompetent. She may control your to-do-list, filling it with "have tos" and "shoulds." And if you fail to complete them, she may leave you feeling guilty and disappointed in yourself. At times she may make you feel alone and isolated. Mostly she tries to fix you, change you, perfect you, and tell you all the ways in which you're not good enough.

It seems to you that she speaks the truth. But come close. I have a secret: your Inner Critic is actually just deceiving you about who you really are.

Your IC sits on her throne in your head, a malignant queen treating you like a loyal but, at times, worthless subject. She tricks you into believing what she's offering you is true, and you listen to everything she's saying because she sounds so much like you. You think, "If she's (I'm) saying it, well then, it must be the truth."

But what if it's not? What if this Queen Critic is nothing but a computer-like program that runs so automatically that you think it's the real you? What if these thoughts that keep popping into your head 24/7 have completely bamboozled you?

This is where freedom begins, with the realization that your Inner Critic is nothing but a fraud, a wolf in sheep's clothing. She doesn't speak the truth, in fact, quite the opposite. She's been feeding you lies as far back as you can remember, lies you've unconsciously programmed into your reality. Her lies make up the way you see yourself, and the way you see the world. They're debilitating, and they paralyze and prevent you from transforming your life and relationships in a meaningful way.

Contrary to what you've subconsciously believed, your IC can't be trusted or relied upon as your guide. But this is exactly who you've been counting on to help you navigate your life.

The good news is that while you will never be able to completely silence her (she's an indelible part of your own programming), you can learn how to live your life from an entirely different perspective. A quote from William Blake sums this up brilliantly: "If the doors of perception were cleansed, everything would appear to man as it is, infinite. For man has closed himself up, till he sees all things through narrow chinks of his cavern."

You have been living in a cavern and thinking it's a castle!

GETTING TO KNOW THE VOICE

When you learn to hear your Inner Critic for the distortionist she really is, you can see that what she thinks of you is actually fiction. That paves the way for you to connect to who you *really* are, so you can feel the way you want to feel and live the life you truly want to live.

Your Inner Critic is the voice that tells you that you just have to be some way other than you are. Start this. Stop that. Act this way, be that way, do anything and everything you can to avoid judgment, criticism, or rejection. Essentially, your IC tells you, over and over again, "You are not enough – and here's why."

If you start paying attention, you may start to recognize that she is never without something to say. In fact, she chimes in right as you wake up:

I have to answer that email from Kim! It's been a week – she probably thinks I'm a total flake. I really have to get organized and get back to people the same day. Oh no! I have to pick up that birthday gift for Amanda's friend! When am I going to fit that in? Ughhhh! This house is such a mess! Why doesn't anyone ever clean up after themselves around here? This outfit looks horrible on me. I can't believe I ate that huge piece of chocolate cake last night. What was I thinking?! Today I'll eat nothing but rice cakes and vegetables!

You blindly listen to this nonstop running commentary, you allow it to determine how you see yourself, and then you project it onto how you think others see you. Sadly, you're so used to living with this voice and letting it drive your day that you can't even imagine a life without it.

But you don't have to keep listening without discernment. Instead, you can start to see her and hear her for who she is. This is your Queen Inner Critic, sitting on her virtual throne and dictating your day to you. She tries to ensure that everything always goes the way that you – and she – want it to. And every time you don't match the perfect picture of who you think you should be, she's right there to tell you what to fix, change, or perfect so that you can be ideal.

Your IC determines your sense of competence as a mother, partner, sister, daughter, friend, or woman. She chimes in to dictate your feelings about your successes, accomplishments, failures, and your body image. She's everywhere – and there isn't a woman (or person, for that matter) alive who escapes her. Even those who appear confident and capable, who seem to have it all together, have an Inner Critic who chides them to be more of this or that. When I ask women at my speaking engagements who among them hears a critical voice in their head, every hand in the audience goes up.

Your IC measures your worth by what others think of you because, in her view, it's the outside world who tells you who you are. So if you can get people to like you, accept you, and agree that you are smart enough, pretty enough, successful enough, and good enough, then you'll be happy. All you need to do, according to the Queen of your mind, is just keep fixing, managing, and pushing yourself to reach this idealized version of you and your life. Then all will be right with your world.

But think about it: Haven't you been listening to this voice for your entire life? And have you ever achieved that perfection? No. Why? Because the minute you attain a goal that your Inner Critic has set for you, you suddenly hear her voice commanding you to strive for the next thing.

Listen to how she talks to you:

"You forgot to pick up the dry cleaning again! You're an idiot," she scolds as you walk up to your front door without your clean clothes.

"The boss thinks you're stupid. You can just tell by the way he looked at you," she says pityingly, even though your boss said no such thing and has never given you reason to believe it.

It doesn't matter how successful you are, how much money you have, how attractive you are, or how much confidence you have. Your IC sees you as failing to measure up.

Why are you listening? Why do you hang on every word, try to meet every demand, and try to match her ideal picture?

That, it turns out, is a very good question.

SHE SOUNDS A LOT LIKE ME

Most people never come to understand that they're actually separate from the voice of the Inner Critic. After all, she's lived inside your mind for your entire life without you knowing she was there. Instead, you mistakenly thought she was *you*. You've heard her for so long that she's become the automatic and habitual way that you think, all day, every day. Just like your body breathes for you without your consciously telling it to, your mind automatically goes to the voice of your Inner Critic without your awareness that it's doing so.

Your six-year-old Inner Critic told you that your mom loved your sister more than you. Your twelve-year-old IC told you that you weren't as smart as Susie. Your sixteen-year-old IC made you feel that you weren't popular enough. And, perhaps, a twenty-five-year-old version said you weren't successful enough at your job.

No matter how old you are or what you do or don't do, the message of "not good enough" plays like a broken record. No wonder many women tell me they wish they had an on-off switch for their minds.

The thing is, they do. And so do you. That on-off switch you yearn for comes from holding the awareness that you and your Inner Critic are separate. Recognizing the difference between the two of you is the key to finding inner peace, joy, and fulfillment.

THE GOOD, THE BAD, AND THE UGLY

You have high expectations for yourself, but no matter how much you accomplish, you find that the bar keeps rising. It's those expectations that may lead you to ask, as many of my clients do, whether the IC is actually a bad thing. "What if the voice motivates me?" they wonder. "What if the voice pushes me to accomplish things?"

But your Inner Critic doesn't typically challenge you to reach satisfying goals. She's more likely to push you toward perfectionism. While that can, indeed, drive you to success, it also breeds a sense of insecurity, inadequacy, and self-doubt. No matter what degree of success you achieve, your IC is there to remind you that whatever you've accomplished so far isn't enough. Her endless criticism creates a pattern of anxiety and chronic dissatisfaction, as today's accomplishments quickly become yesterday's news.

Dethroning Your Inner Critic gives you the tools to take guidance from a different mind, one that speaks from self-love, self-acknowledgement, self-compassion, and self-empowerment. This is transformational. You can take risks and speak your truth, knowing that you will still be loved and accepted. You can learn from your mistakes and failures without judgment. You can recognize that you are no different than any other human being on the planet – after all, no one escapes the grip of the Inner Critic.

You don't have to worry about shutting her up or making her go away. She's an automatic, reflexive part of your brain, and ridding yourself of her is impossible. Happily, all you have to do is learn how to stop listening to her.

You might be reading this book because you know you wouldn't talk to a friend the way you talk to yourself, but you don't know how to stop the automatic mind chatter. You might be in search of greater satisfaction in your life. You may worry about making mistakes, or have difficulty making decisions. You might be avoiding taking action to create what you *really* want in your life because you're afraid of failure, getting stuck in your head, or overthinking your choices.

DYIC will show you how to stop your Inner Critic from sabotaging yourself, whipping up fear, and keeping you from the life you are meant to be living. You'll learn how to stop worrying about what people think of you, getting recognition from others, or avoiding failure, rejection, and judgment. You'll no longer have need for excuses that limit your potential. You'll break the habit of listening to your IC, even when she's screaming at you.

When you know how to dethrone your Inner Critic, you'll have the power to trade your fear and anxiety in for excitement. You'll discover an unlimited capacity for love and abundance. You'll learn a whole new way of thinking that will, quite simply, transform your life.

CHAPTER TWO

HOW I GOT OFF
THE MERRY-GO-ROUND

I'm a psychotherapist, author, podcaster, public speaker, and workshop facilitator. But my Inner Critic has never stopped screaming at me, even with every step I take to get this message out to the world. Whether I'm leading a workshop for twenty women or two hundred, my IC says the same thing: "This has already been said a thousand different ways by a thousand different authors who are famous, life-changing gurus. What makes you think you have what it takes to make that kind of impact on the world?"

Ouch.

I practice dethroning my Inner Critic every day. In fact, the only reason you're reading this is because my lifelong personal work has been to detach from her.

My Inner Critic's warnings and attempts to "protect" me from the judgment and rejection of others began very early in my life. When I was a shy kid in elementary school, she told me I'd better stay quiet or other kids would make fun of me. It only took some minor teasing from boys in my class about my red hair and having the maiden name Fox to assure me that she was right, and plant her firmly on her throne. From that point on, my IC would only let me come out of my shell when she knew for sure that I'd be accepted.

I spent my childhood and adolescence struggling to find inner peace, but I didn't know why I found it elusive. On all fronts, I had a fantastic life. I had loving parents, wonderful friends, good health, boyfriends, and a middle-class sense of security. Why, then, did I frequently feel I was somehow not good enough?

I became a seeker, and in 1989, when I was nineteen, I attended a six-day retreat in the hopes it would lead me to more happiness. One of the retreat's challenges was a ropes course designed to force participants to confront their fears. I stood on a platform the size of a dinner plate mounted a hundred feet in the air. My instructions? Simply step off.

Although I knew intellectually that my safety harness would keep me safe, that knowledge didn't unglue my feet from that dinner plate for almost half an hour. Finally, something within me swelled up and took the form of a thought. "Don't let fear stop you," it said.

I was still scared to death. But even so, shaking and crying, I stepped off the platform. And with this simple action came an epiphany that would forever change the course of my life: *Who gives a f*@k if you're scared?*

It would be quite a few more years before I realized how fully I was being run by what I would come to identify as my Inner Critic, someone whose voice was not my own. But it was the start of questioning my thoughts. And so I began to experiment. What would happen if, instead of listening to the voice telling me to stay in my comfort zone (stay small, don't take risks), I listened to a different part of myself (don't let fear stop you)?

The results were pretty phenomenal. Within a short time, I started talking to people I would have never talked to before. I joined a club lacrosse team, even though I was absolutely terrible at lacrosse. I started showing up in the world as a confident person. I started meeting new people, having more fun, and feeling calmer in my daily life. At twenty-one, I felt confident enough to move to New Orleans, where I didn't know a soul, to pursue my graduate degree. All because of the question I would ask myself over and over: *Who gives a f*@k if you're scared?*

THE MERRY-GO-ROUND OF LIFE

I may have gotten over being scared, but I was still hooked by my Inner Critic. I became a successful psychotherapist. I had a husband who loved me. I had three healthy kids and wonderful friends. I'd been courageous. I'd taken risks. I was grateful for all I had, but it still felt like something wasn't right. Why was I *still* not happy?

It took me a while to realize that I had made my happiness contingent upon externals. My clients needed to think I was brilliant. My kids needed to be doing great. My husband needed to sweep me off my feet every day, and my vacations needed to be the envy of my circle. I had these pictures of what a perfect life looked like, and my Inner Critic told me the only way I could be happy was if my life matched them.

Life would be good, she promised me, if only I was the weight I needed to be, my practice was where it should be, my marriage was in good shape, my recent lecture/workshop went really well, and I was the fun one everyone could count on to be the life of the party. If there was anything off in any of these areas, my IC would repeat, once again, that I was just not good enough.

This inner turmoil was a vulnerability I hid from the world. I was sure that if I wasn't "enough," I wouldn't be loved, valued, or accepted. I'd created an exhausting, vicious cycle that meant I needed to achieve more and more in order to chase happiness: more new friends, more exciting vacations, more personal and professional success.

Now, I'm going to cut myself some slack here. I was and am a child of our culture, just as you are. And, unfortunately, that culture teaches us that our emotions are created by the circumstances of our lives. I, like so many others, was on the merry-go-round of trying to fix, change, or perfect myself – my circumstances, my weight, my spouse, my children, my career. This, I'd been tacitly taught, was how to be happy.

But since the joy, contentment, and peace I craved weren't about my circumstances, those feelings remained unattainable. Instead, I lived in a state of anxiety, overwhelm, and frustration, feelings that determined my behavior toward myself and the people around me.

Because I was demanding of myself, I was demanding of everyone. My husband and kids found me critical – and I could hardly blame them. It wasn't until I began to identify that voice, the voice of my Inner Critic, that I began to see that my mind had been scurrying around, finding all of those places where nothing was ever good enough, for pretty much my entire life. I realized that as long as I allowed the IC and my mind to run amok, I would continue to be restless and miserable.

TAKING CONTROL OF MY MIND

This is how I began to start to become aware of, and then break the habit of listening to, the critical voice within. When I stopped believing what she said, my whole life began to shift. It became crystal clear that the only way I could feel the way I wanted was by learning that I was in control of the thoughts I chose to listen to. I understood, finally, that my quality of life was something I could choose, in any and every moment, by deciding how I wanted to think.

This meant examining the thoughts and beliefs that I'd thought were simply *me* my whole life and figuring out who, if they weren't mine, they belonged to. I realized that my mind, like yours, was conditioned to repeat certain thoughts and feelings on a repetitive loop. It was this conditioned, habitual voice in the mind that I named the Inner Critic.

I learned what worked and what didn't. For example, I wasn't able to change what my Inner Critic said or stop her from nattering. This is why I don't call the work that I do in the world "Silencing the Inner Critic" or "Banishing the Inner Critic" – neither are possible. I discovered that trying to make myself feel better by stifling those reflexive, automatic thoughts was a set-up.

It's like me telling you not to think about pink elephants. Go on, try to not think about pink elephants after I've repeated the words "pink elephants" several times. I'll bet you're trying with all your might not to think about pink elephants right now.

The goal, I realized, was instead to break the habit of giving energy and attention to the Inner Critic conditioning. This required moment-to-moment awareness of my thoughts. Then, instead of resisting or trying to change those thoughts and the feelings that accompanied them, I simply allowed them to be. I let my unhappy emotions be my mirror, so I could see what I was thinking that made me feel distressed.

At first, I felt resistance. Most of us avoid uncomfortable emotions by using distraction, numbing behaviors, and denial to escape having to deal with them. But learning to feel all my emotions, not just the ones I liked, was key to dethroning the Inner Critic.

We are what we think about. I am, and so are you. I learned that I needed to be highly aware of what I thought about so I could catch myself when I found my thoughts going to what was missing in my life, where I was falling short, and what others thought of me.

When my Inner Critic was running amok on autopilot, she had a litany of so many things that I supposedly *needed* for my happiness. For a long time, I was completely blind to this. And because I was blind, I had no idea that I was a control freak. A perfectionist.

In the past, I would never have considered myself a perfectionist. I don't have the perfect home. I don't push my kids to be perfect. In fact, most people who know me would say that I'm pretty laid back and positive. But as I listened to my repetitive thoughts, I realized that if the unending theme song of my Inner Critic was that nothing was ever good enough, then I was indeed chasing perfection.

And that was mostly how my life went. Sure, I had many glimpses of gratitude, joy, fulfillment, and peace. But they never lasted. My Inner Critic was always looking for what was next.

How could I make sure my kids were happy? How could I make sure that I was a great mom? How could I make sure I was an amazing psychotherapist? How could I make sure that my husband appreciated me? How make my home the environment that I wanted it to be?

Those thoughts kept me always striving, always reaching, always wanting more – and always feeling unsettled. But once I started engaging with those thoughts as nothing more than the habitual conditioning of my Inner Critic, I saw that I could choose to ignore them.

The thoughts still come! I can't change that. But I can decide to observe them without following them. Dethroning my Inner Critic has meant I can stop focusing on what I fear is missing and instead shift my thoughts toward who I already am, what I already have, and the conviction that everything I need is already inside of me.

My thoughts of worry, fear, and inadequacy were so familiar I didn't even see them as something I could pick up or put down. But understanding that I have choice and control over what I think has been a game-changer.

In the following chapters, you'll learn how to practice having different thoughts on purpose, about what happened in your past, about your current circumstances, and about how your future will unfold. As Wayne Dyer used to say, "When you change the way you look at things, the things you look at change."

Dethroning Your Inner Critic is about nothing less than changing who you've known yourself to be and, by extension, every aspect of your life.

CHAPTER THREE

DO YOU SEE WHAT I SEE?

No matter how you spend your days, or, for that matter, how you spend your life, your Inner Critic tells you all the ways in which you're falling short. You're not good enough. In fact you aren't enough, period. You need to fix this, change that, stop this thing, and do this other thing. And that's just for starters.

Hold up here. You already *are* enough. There is nothing to fix, change, or perfect about you or your life. Being enough isn't about anything you do or don't do. You are enough because you are alive. Your purpose is being *you*, your Authentic Self. The only one examining your life to make sure you are good enough is your Inner Critic, and she's irrelevant. There is nothing you need to be, do, or have to be whole.

Because you are already whole, you have no need for some weird Inner Critic calling you out every moment of every day. Once your IC is no longer in the driver's seat, trying to fix, change, and perfect you, you are *free*. All of a sudden, there is wide, open space for you to examine what's possible that would make your life more enjoyable. Life stops being about fixing, and becomes something that can generate excitement and vitality. This is what makes life worth living.

Released from the tyranny of your Inner Critic, you can grow, evolve, learn, and create something different just because it makes life more fun and worthwhile – not because there is something broken or not good enough. When you know you're already enough, you can learn to see your fear, your failures, and your experiences of rejection through a new lens. The journey of transforming your life is lined with a lot of these feelings that can make you feel really uncomfortable. And that's okay. Wouldn't you rather feel uncomfortable while going for your dreams than feel uncomfortable because you're not?

Awareness is everything. Once you see when and how your IC shows up, you'll be able to keep her from taking charge of your thoughts, feelings, and experiences. *You* will be the author of the thoughts you allow to rule your mind. You'll interrupt the thinking you've previously accepted as normal.

You will rewire your mind to reject the warped advice of your IC. And because you will have a rewired mind designing your life moving forward, you will actually learn to alter the parts of your personality that were formed by your IC.

Rewiring your mind sounds complex, but it's actually quite simple. By following the steps and tools in this book, you'll learn how to separate yourself from your IC the moment she acts up – and how to choose and focus on different thoughts instead. The result? You'll be able to hear the thoughts of the *real* you. The Authentic Self that lies hidden within you, trapped underneath your IC.

THE M.I.N.D. METHOD

Dethroning Your Inner Critic is a four-step process I call the M.I.N.D. Method. In the coming chapters, I'll take you through each step in detail so that you can get to know each of them, one at a time. Then it's simply a matter of practicing each step every day. When you master these steps and the concepts behind them, you'll have the opportunity to live a more rewarding and exceptional life. You'll also have the ability to share this information with others – especially the next generation. Wouldn't it be great if this exhausting, unconscious habit of self-narration and self-criticism stopped with you, rather than spreading to your kids?

M: Meet Your Inner Critic

The M Step, Meet Your Inner Critic, brings you face to face with your Inner Critic on a daily basis. Getting to know her intimately is what will help you break her grip. You will start to know exactly when it is her speaking, and what has triggered her rants. You will be able to instantly release her grip as soon as you know her voice.

I: Investigate the Indication Signs

Investigating what I call the Indication Signs will allow you to see all of ways your Inner Critic signals that she's sitting high up on the throne in your mind. You'll be able to spot all of the emotions, body sensations, and behaviors that serve as blaring red warning signs that she is back in power.

N: Neutralize the Never-Ending Messages

While it may initially seem like the IC changes up what she says and how she advises you, you'll see that once you drill down, her nagging always comes down to the same broken record. Your Inner Critic has always had the same attachments throughout your life. The only thing that has changed are her attempted solutions to satisfy those attachments.

D: Design Your Life

Once you've begun to free yourself from the IC's grip, you'll be able to envision a new future to step into. In this step, we'll imagine the possibilities that await you when you are no longer being governed by your Inner Critic.

The idea of Dethroning Your Inner Critic is to interrupt the automatic habit of giving your energy and attention to your Inner Critic mind. When you practice DYIC on a daily basis, you are moving into a new mind. You are rewiring your thoughts and changing the way you feel. As a result, you'll begin taking action consistent with your new thoughts. Those new thoughts will transform your life into one you're designing instead of defaulting to.

At any given moment, you can either be a host to your most powerful, rewarding and fulfilling life, or you can be a hostage of your Inner Critic. The choice is yours. Once you learn the skills you need to dethrone your Inner Critic, you will live a happier and more productive life. And when you are leading your life from a place of authenticity, instead of your Inner Critic's voice, you have the key to living even beyond the life of your dreams.

$\mathcal{M}$

MEET YOUR INNER CRITIC

It has always been easy to hate and destroy;
to build and to cherish is much more difficult.
QUEEN ELIZABETH II

As I've said, most of my clients tell me they just want to be happy. And most of them are looking for things outside themselves to deliver that happiness to them – just as I once did.

You've probably done this too. You may have spent most of your life so far chasing happiness through your relationships, your career, your bank account, or your body. You may have thought, "Once I have the perfect relationship, then I will be happy," or, "Once I have children, then I will be happy," or even, "Once I make this much money, then I will be happy."

But these reflexive, circumstance-based thoughts about happiness – that it's a permanent state of being dependent upon meeting specific external milestones and goals – mean you're likely to find true happiness elusive.

Where do these thoughts come from? Likely they're recycled thoughts passed on to you by your parents, your parents' parents, and our culture, and adopted and pushed on you by your Inner Critic. You don't realize you're not thinking your own thoughts, nor have you even learned how to think your own thoughts. Given that your mind speaks to you incessantly, this is a big problem!

Research shows that on average, you, like the rest of us, talk to yourself in your head a staggering 50,000 times a day, mostly *about* you. With so much time focused on your thoughts, it's no wonder that you think what's going on in your mind is the same as what's going on in the external world. It feels normal and natural. Your body breathes for you, your heart beats for you, and your mind thinks for you. You don't tell your mind where to focus. It's on autopilot.

It's your Inner Critic who runs this show, centering your thoughts on the parts of you and your life that don't match her ideal. No matter how much of your life has been working just fine – accomplishments like finishing school or finding our first job, love of family and friends – your IC says you need something different, something more.

Since she is never satisfied, you can't be satisfied, not as long as you cannot see yourself as independent of her. Your life will continue to feel as if something's missing. That's why the very first step in the M.I.N.D. Method is M: Meet Your Inner Critic. You can't hear her if you don't know who she is and the difference between her voice and your own.

THE DESPOT QUEEN VS THE AUTHENTIC SELF

But wait. If you're not your Queen Inner Critic, the voice ruling from the throne in your mind, then who are you? What if, you may ask, that voice is telling me the truth? Shouldn't I listen to it sometimes?

Maybe. Maybe not. Before you listen to the voice in your head, it's critical to determine whether that voice is coming from your Inner Critic or your Authentic Self (AS). Here's a hint: your Authentic Self is who shows up when your Inner Critic is temporarily absent.

The AS can feel elusive. For most of us, this kind of authenticity isn't a permanent state, but something we practice returning to. I call it the Authentic Self, but philosophers, theologians, and gurus have given it many names, many words, and many expressions over centuries, none of which are the absolute truth. The best you can do is to point to something: a space, a feeling, an energy, a vibration, a stillness, a peace. Whatever its name, it is a sense of being present to something true or honest that touches you in a way that's different from your normal reality. I heard my Authentic Self on that dinner plate-sized platform in the thought, "Don't let your fear stop you."

Usually, your Authentic Self is swallowed whole by the constant chatter of your IC. And so the real work is to build the muscle that separates you from that nonstop humming so you can experience yourself when your Inner Critic is silent. Therein lies the choice: to practice again and again separating yourself from the Inner Critic who presently runs your life, and begin experimenting with that which appears in the absence of that incessantly controlling voice.

Access to your Authentic Self comes from the ability to quiet that voice and discover what lies behind your mind-made story. Our unhappiness stems from the habit of allowing our Inner Critic to run our lives. When we access our Authentic Selves, we are accessing that part of ourselves that is not defined by our jobs, our roles, or what others think of us. It is the composite of your wisdom, your gifts that you bring to the world, and all of the things that are uniquely yours and need expression, rather than what you believe you are supposed to be and do. When you have access to your Authentic Self, then, and only then, can you truly feel the way you want to feel and live the life you want to live.

When you learn to spot the difference between your IC and you, you have the power to no longer pay attention to her or take guidance from her. Once you get into the routine of practicing the M.I.N.D. Method every day, you'll be able to take on anything you're struggling with – weight, career, finances, children, relationships, resentment from the past, worry about the future – and resolve it.

Here are some ways to identify the Despot Queen, your Inner Critic:

- She's mean, harsh, and critical
- Her stories are repetitive, like a broken record
- She tells you that you need to change in order to feel the way you want
- She's constantly comparing you to others
- Everything she says is black and white (you're either amazing or you suck) with very little evidence to back either up
- She is the voice of "shoulds" and "you can't be happy until ..." or "because ..."
- Her programing keeps you stalled in self-doubt and self-criticism rather than self-care

Your Authentic Self, however, feels more like this:

- You give your desires more attention than your fears
- You let your creative juices flow
- You see challenges as a platform for your own growth
- Your intention is always to get curious and gather data rather than make quick assessments and judgments

The differences might be easier to hear in action. In the passages below, a woman wants desperately to become a life coach and start a new career. She is doubting herself: unsure and hesitant.

Inner Critic speaking:

I would love to become a life coach. But I don't know the first thing about running a business. Where would I get my clients from? Who would pay me? I should have done this when I was young and single. Now everyone's a coach, and there's too much competition out there. I'll never be able to be financially successful. I just don't have what it takes.

Authentic Self speaking:

I would love to become a life coach. I would love to help people learn to live their best lives and be their best selves. Plus, I would love the independence and challenge. I feel that it's what I'm meant to do, and I really want to support my family financially. I wonder how I could find out what's needed and see how that fits with where I am? I'll start researching how to become a life coach this week. This feels scary and risky, but I'm excited and committed to figuring out what it will take to create a new future for myself.

Here's another example from a woman who would love for her marriage to have more connection and companionship.

Inner Critic speaking:

I feel that we can have a better relationship, but he seems fine with the way things are. He's not going to do anything about it. This is just who he is, so I guess this is as good as it gets. I am just not that kind of affectionate person. And people who have that kind of connection are people who have more in common with each other, and they're just different from us. I knew this when I married him. Nothing will ever change, so accept what you've got.

Authentic Self speaking:

I feel that we can have a better relationship, but he seems fine with the way things are. Hmmm ... maybe he wants a better relationship too. Maybe he doesn't know how I'm feeling. What could I do to create a better relationship with him? What would I need to do to make that happen? This could be exciting and thrilling! I'm going to do whatever it takes on my end to make this happen. Even if it feels weird, uncomfortable, or even a little scary, I'm really committed to making this happen.

Notice that when the Authentic Self takes the wheel, you can hear curiosity, investigation, creativity, and generative thinking, as opposed to the Inner Critic, who reinforces fear and complacency. Authentic Self thinking leads to action because the Inner Critic isn't blocking the path forward.

It's of note that, in both examples, the Authentic Self is much more rational and open to possibility. There is an interest in real information-gathering. There is a focus on the topic itself – not on the IC's concern about worthiness or "good enough."

Now let's meet *your* Inner Critic.

WHICH QUEEN RULES YOU?

Your Inner Critic sits in your mind like a queen on her throne. She may be subtle or she may speak harshly, but no matter how your Inner Critic sounds, her goal is to rule over you. Which of these Queens can you relate to?

Queen Bad Girl
Theme Song: "If You Don't Succeed, You Suck"
She makes you feel unlovable, flawed, inferior, incompetent, and inadequate. She says harsh, nasty things to you, the kinds of things you'd never say to anyone else, because she believes the meaner she is to you, the more motivated you will be to change. She sees life as very black and white: You are either pretty or ugly. You are either smart or stupid. Fat or thin. You are a great mom or a bad mom. There is really no in-between with Queen Bad Girl.
Queen Wishy Washy
Theme Song: "I Dunno, What Do You Think?"
She rules with fear and anxiety, making you feel dependent on others, vulnerable, and worried about losing control, being

abandoned, or feeling isolated. This is the IC who makes you say yes even when you really mean no, and wants you to sacrifice everything to accommodate your children, your friends, your work. She's all about making sure you won't be judged or criticized, because then, she reasons, you'll never have to feel bad about yourself. The end result is that you either remain in indecision or defer to the opinions of others.

Queen Inadequate
Theme Song: "Try Harder"

It's too bad, she says, that you don't put in more effort – because you could do and be better. "The house could be cleaner," she says. Or, "You look alright, but you could stand to lose five more pounds – and you should really be able to hold a plank for two minutes." She keeps you quiet at the staff meeting because your idea is "okay," but not really ready to present to your boss yet. Even if life is pretty good, she says, it's not at the level that it could be. She keeps you in constant restless striving by pointing out the areas where you could be better than you are. No matter what you've accomplished, you're just not cutting it. Your every effort is inferior or insufficient.

Queen Perfectionist
Theme Song: "If It's Not Perfect, It's Ruined"

This queen is a control freak, making constant demands and shaming you for not meeting her crazy standards. Think Mommy Dearest. This Queen writes outrageously critical narratives about every aspect of your life: your career, your parenting, your looks, your personality traits, your relationships. You know exactly how life should be – you can see it in magazines, on social media, on TV. Why can't you ever get it right?!

Queen Guil
Theme Song: "It's All My Fault"

She makes you feel bad about what you have – and haven't – done. She holds onto the past, constantly reminding you of all the times that you've hurt or disappointed someone. She punishes you for what she says you've gotten wrong, and makes you believe that you're a bad person for it. She won't allow you to forgive yourself. You deserve unhappiness. You mess everything up.

Queen Victim
Theme Song: "It's Not My Fault!"

At the other end of the spectrum, this Queen has a pervasive sense of helplessness and will convince you that your life is really, really hard. Oh, woe is me. Boo-hoo. Cry me a river! This IC variant whines and complains about how hard life is for her. She – and you – can't be happy until other people change or treat you better. She makes excuses for why your life doesn't look the way you want it – and it's because of your parents, your ex-husband, your past circumstances, even your genetics. Her reign makes you feel depressed, pessimistic, helpless, and downright hopeless.

IDENTIFYING YOUR QUEEN

Know that there may be aspects of more than one Queen that comprise your unique Inner Critic. Which theme songs, above, sound the most like the persistent thoughts in your head? What underlying messages resonated with you?

Once you have a handle on what she sounds like, close your eyes. And get a picture of what she looks like. Ask yourself:

- What do her facial features look like?
- What kind of expressions does she make?
- What is her body like?
- How does she hold herself?
- What nonverbal cues are you getting from her?
- How does she wear her hair?
- How is she dressed?
- Does she look like anyone you know? Your mother? Your sister? Grandmother?

- Does she have the qualities of your father or another man in your life?

Once you've identified the characteristics and appearance of your IC, meeting her becomes about *observing* her on a daily basis – not silencing her, ignoring her, avoiding her, or running away from her, which is probably what you thought you would learn from this book. Instead, we're doing the opposite. We are becoming intimately familiar with her voice, her tone, her every demand, and her every "should." When you practice observing her, you have the key to breaking free from her grip for the rest of your life.

MEET YOUR INNER CRITIC

These practices are designed to bring you face to face with the voice of your Inner Critic. As you engage in these practices, notice if specific ideas about how you "should" be practicing these tools come up. Is your Inner Critic critiquing and evaluating how this should go? Find some humor and irony in Meeting Your Inner Critic even as she dictates how these meetings are "supposed to" unfold.

Step One: Meditation
Meditation is the practice of intentionally turning your focus away from your automatic thoughts and tuning into a single point of reference such as your breath, a body sensation, a mantra, a sound, or a feeling such as gratitude. For the next seven days, spend at least ten minutes a day meditating. Find a quiet spot where you won't be disturbed – it can even be your car. Remember, meditation is the *practice* of quieting your mind. Many people who begin a meditation practice say they can't stop their mind from thinking. This is perfectly okay and normal. The idea is simply to remain in stillness and observe your thoughts.

Step Two: Thought Log

For the next week, keep a thought log so you can spot your Inner Critic throughout your day. Start by taking ten minutes to journal in the morning before getting out of bed. Mornings matter. When you bring awareness to your IC first thing, you'll be more likely to notice where she shows up later in the day. Get a piece of paper and a pen, close your eyes, and get ready to hear what she has to say. Take your time, and begin to feel the energy inside you when she is speaking to you.

Write down all of the thoughts in your mind. Don't stop. Just write and write and write until there's nothing left to say. When your mind is clogged with the negative chatter of your Inner Critic, it can be very difficult to even see *why* you're feeling the way you are. You can't change what you can't even see.

If you find, while doing this exercise, that you're questioning in your mind whether you're doing it "right," add that second-guessing to the list. It's another sign that your Inner Critic is trying to make it – and you – perfect.

Keep your thought log for seven days and notice how much time you spend listening to your Inner Critic. Is she complaining, judging, and criticizing? Making you or someone else guilty? Is she comparing you to other people, getting angry, being self-righteous, or justifying why you feel the way you do? Is she focusing on the future worse case scenarios that she's inventing? Write it all down.

Step Three: Your Inner Critic Interview

Take a few minutes every day, preferably at the same time, to interview your Inner Critic and list the answers to the following questions. You can return to these questions at any time throughout your journey.

- Where is she causing me to worry?
- What is she saying to me when I first wake up about the day ahead, or about something in my life?

- Where do I feel that I'm not good enough right now?
- Where is she personalizing someone else's behavior?
- Who do I feel hurt or frustrated by?
- Where is she causing chaos in my life?
- Where is she "shoulding" on me?
- Where can I let go of past regret or future worry today?
- What do I need to let go of right now to stay centered and at peace?

Step Four: End-of-Day Wrap-Up

At the end of the day, you may want to revisit your thought log and ask yourself these questions:

- What or who did I get triggered by today?
- When did my IC show up the most and why?
- Where in my day did I listen to my IC?
- If this situation happened again, what thought could I have about the situation that is aligned with my Authentic Self instead of my Inner Critic?

CHAPTER FIVE

I

INVESTIGATE THE INDICATION SIGNS

Now that you know how to Meet Your Inner Critic, how can you prevent her from dragging you into the same old rabbit hole she's been taking you down for as long as you can remember? This is where the **I** Step comes in. Indication Signs are made up of the feelings, urges, impulses, actions, numbing behaviors, addictions, body sensations, and habits that, once identified, serve as warning signs that your Inner Critic has taken over and is ruling your mind.

All of your emotions, positive or negative, are created by your thoughts. And it is your emotions that determine what actions you take in your life. When you feel happy, fulfilled, and peaceful, you act one way. When you are angry, sad, lonely, or ashamed, you act another. Since action is what determines the direction of your life, the only way to go somewhere different is to take different actions – which means practicing different thoughts. The only way to do that is to practice the first step of the M.I.N.D. Method, Meet Your Inner Critic, every day and separate yourself from her rants.

But meeting your IC can be challenging if you're blind to the fact that she's taken over. Like the rest of us, you're probably so used to living with her that you just don't see her in action. Even when you learn to pay attention, life will continue to present plenty of opportunities for your IC to regain power. Life is like that. Half of the time, things go the way you want. But the other half, they don't.

When life doesn't go the way you imagined, how you choose to think is what determines how you feel. By understanding your Indication Signs and paying close attention to the emotions, body sensations, urges, impulses, and behaviors that indicate your IC is stepping into power and reigning over your mind, you can easily distinguish her voice from your own and detach from her demands and expectations.

Indication Signs like sadness, fear, anger, jealousy, shame, and humiliation create sensations inside your body. They also create behaviors such as numbing, avoiding, lashing out, distracting, or escaping. These are all warnings that can alert you to conditioned, reflexive thinking.

You know those days where all you want to do is lie in bed and binge watch Netflix? How about those times when you want to drink a whole bottle of wine, or eat an entire chocolate brownie tray, or fire off a nasty email to a co-worker, or scream at the person who just cut you off in traffic? Those might be Indication Signs that your IC has stirred up some drama. In order to change our lives, we need to be willing to use these moments as our greatest teacher. We need to get curious and investigate the old, programmed thoughts from our IC that cause us to feel and act this way.

Let's take a look at this in action. My client Eileen is a brilliant example of how to use Indication Signs to create freedom and joy. She's an executive at a prominent NYC management consulting firm and puts in long hours working with CEOs, many of them men. Eileen struggled with binge eating for most of her adult life, and also with drinking too much wine in the evening. She'd been able to get both under control, but not for long. She felt they were in the way of her living her best life.

I surprised Eileen by telling her I wanted her to stop focusing on her eating and drinking entirely. She protested. "If I don't pay attention to my eating or drinking, then I will *really* become a huge, gluttonous mess," she said. After some assurance, though, she was willing to trust me and begin the daily work of meeting her Inner Critic.

At first, Eileen found meditating challenging. Her mind would race, and she caught herself thinking about her to-do list for the day. But I encouraged her to stick with it and pay attention to her body sensations. By day three, she began to notice the tension in her shoulders (an Indication Sign) and focused on relaxing them. Once she relaxed her shoulders during meditation, she was able to practice this at the office.

Eileen's morning brain dump, written in her journal, shocked her by revealing that, while she felt good about herself as a smart, accomplished woman, she was angry at and judgmental of many of the men she worked with. She thought they considered themselves smarter, better, and more capable than she, and she often complained in her journal about feeling demeaned. Eileen began to see the automatic thoughts that whipped her up into frustration, resentment, and sometimes outright rage, and she felt the tension in her stomach just reading them (another Indication Sign).

Prior to recognizing that this was the voice of her IC, she felt justified in her thoughts about her colleagues. She had no idea how much power she was giving away by allowing other people's behavior to make her feel demeaned, inadequate, and less than – Queen Victim was in play. Her body sensations, her anger, and her self-righteousness were all warning signs that Eileen's IC was sitting high up on the throne of her mind.

With the newfound recognition of her IC, Eileen began to see herself from a completely new perspective, watching herself in her anger as an observer of the emotion rather than getting sucked in. It was this simple witnessing that created a space between Eileen and her autopilot Inner Critic mind. She no longer had to resist the feelings of frustration and rage. She could simply be with them.

No longer triggered at work into a firestorm of negative thoughts, she was able to see that she'd been bringing her anger home. She would look around the house, furious over all the repairs that needed to get done. She would yell at her kids for leaving dirty dishes in the living room. And after a long day of this kind of intense negative reactivity, she would numb herself with food and alcohol.

For the first time, Eileen clearly saw that binge-eating and drinking were accidental byproducts of her IC's internal dialogue. She also saw that her Indication Signs – the emotions, body sensations, and behaviors – were the same whether she was upset about a colleague dismissing her accomplishments or about the bathroom that needed a fresh coat of paint. Either way, she felt that she wasn't good enough. Here, Queen Inadequate demanded to be heard.

Unable to control the world, Eileen turned to trying to gain control over her food and alcohol consumption. Once she saw this coping mechanism for what it was and stopped numbing with food and alcohol, she became intimately familiar with the broken record theme song of her IC. She stopped resisting her negative emotions, and instead turned toward them. Using her Indication Signs of irritability, frustration, anger, and judgment as powerful tools for self-growth, she learned exactly when to tune into the voice in her mind – and when not to.

After seven months, Eileen had dropped almost forty pounds and was drinking alcohol only on social occasions.

When you Investigate the Indication Signs, you get curious about the drama your IC whips up in her determination to fix your life, other people, and, most of all, you. Silencing her doesn't work and doesn't help, and neither does stuffing uncomfortable feelings by trying to numb, distract, or avoid. True freedom comes from feeling all your feelings.

Paying attention to your Indication Signs – your thoughts, emotions, behaviors, and body sensations – exposes your Inner Critic and creates the possibility for a whole new world to open up. You stop running away from the half of life you have not wanted to feel. Instead of trying to be happy all of the time, you are willing to feel the discomfort that is the necessary price of growth. When you are willing to embrace the other half of life that comes with the hard and painful emotions, you have the power to make all of your dreams come true. You are able to embrace the possibility of failure, and have the courage to try. You can risk rejection, pain, shame, disappointment, and fear instead of always trying to fight against these feelings.

Imagine the freedom of designing a future where you no longer have to fear failure, rejection or judgment! Instead of shrinking in situations that your IC says are dangerous, imagine what might happen if you could take more risks, keep your heart open with anyone you meet, and take actions that are in alignment with the life you want to create. When you are able to use your Indication Signs as a signal to separate yourself from your IC's demands and expectations, you are free.

Try this mindset shift: When things come up in life that are painful, reframe it as a *challenge* instead of letting your Inner Critic turn it into a problem. What is happening in the present moment may cause you discomfort, but it's only a problem when you identify with what your Inner Critic says about the experience. If you are investigating the Indication Signs and using them to your benefit, your discomfort is simply another tool for growth.

Your Inner Critic has always judged certain feelings and circumstances as negative. You have aligned with her complaints, and that has become your experience of yourself, your life, what happened in your past, and what should or shouldn't be happening in your future. And when all of this negativity is ruling your mind, you probably find a lot of ways to avoid the vulnerability that it brings.

One of the most profound and transformational examples of using the Dethroning Your Inner Critic methods and going for a life of your dreams is my client Gabrielle, who had been in and out of rehab, seen multiple addiction counselors, and participated in Narcotics Anonymous, but had been unable to break her addiction. In desperation, her father connected Gabrielle to me, even though I'm not an addictions therapist.

Gabrielle had grown up in an affluent neighborhood and attended a competitive high school. She'd struggled in school due to some learning challenges, and suffered from intense anxiety because she felt like she wasn't measuring up to who she thought she was supposed to be. In her early teen years, she fell in with the wrong crowd and began using drugs as a way of coping with her intense feelings of inadequacy. By the time I met her, she was a full-blown heroin addict. She had kicked drugs several times, but every time she got clean, the anxiety was so overwhelming that she did nothing but sleep all day and stay up all night playing video games.

Gabrielle told me that she'd only agreed to see me to humor her father, and she didn't think anything we did would work – she expected to die a heroin addict. But Gabrielle and I didn't focus on what had happened in the past like her previous counselors did. Instead, we worked on identifying the persistent thoughts of her Inner Critic.

"When you told me that I didn't have to change or fix any of the old thoughts I was having, but that everything my mind was telling me was nothing more than a computer-programmed message from my Inner Critic, that was the game changer," Gabrielle confided in me later. "You told me to make sure that my new thoughts and actions were in alignment with the new life that I wanted to create, and it never left my head. I will still have cravings for heroin, but then I will ask myself, 'Is getting high in alignment with my new life?' and just that one thing has saved my life."

Gabrielle's Inner Critic had convinced her that she deserved to hate herself (hello, Queen Bad Girl). But freed from her IC's tyranny, she grew able to see her own value, and to stop comparing herself to idealized pictures of what she was supposed to be. She learned to feel love not just for herself, but for others.

"The greatest part of this work is that when you have a sense of love for yourself, it's not hard *not* to want to f*ck your life up," she told me. "Now that I love myself, which I *never* thought was possible, I don't want to ruin my life, and if I get uncomfortable, I now know how to get through it."

As I write this, Gabrielle will be a year clean from heroin, and is enrolled in college to get a degree as a drug counselor. Her goal is to get certified to teach other addicts to dethrone their Inner Critics.

Gabrielle, like many, had seen her conditioned IC thoughts as facts, but a life-saving shift occurred when she became willing to take action from a different mind, a *rewired* mind. She's still uncomfortable every time she steps out of her comfort zone and risks rejection, failure, and judgment, but she now knows that she can sit with the discomfort she used to numb with drugs and sleep.

When we confuse the automatic thoughts of the Inner Critic for reality, we don't realize that those thoughts represent a biased view of life, our relationships, and ourselves. But your Indication Signs can reveal the highly subjective nature of your IC's interpretations of the world around you. Some of those interpretations might have even formed parts of your personality.

Uncomfortable emotions are a part of life. They're unavoidable. But when you try to control or ward off those feelings, as Eileen did by eating and drinking, you're unable to see the connection between your thoughts, your feelings, and your actions. Consider that emotions are nothing more than vibrations inside the body. Instead of avoiding the ones you think are painful and negative, sitting with them allows you to see why you do what you do – and choose otherwise.

We have the choice to either learn to feel all of our emotions and see life's challenges as an opportunity to grow, or we can be afraid of these challenges and then spend our lives trying to avoid or prevent things from happening that seem frightening.

I would rather learn to feel all of my emotions. My emotions are my Indication Signs that my Inner Critic is at it again, assigning meaning to something going on in my life and making me feel that I am not good enough. And when I don't feel good enough, I get irritable, easily frustrated, and very critical of myself and the people closest to me. I also get tired, and I don't want to be around anyone. I don't want to be social, and I don't have the energy to exercise my body.

My Inner Critic is Queen Perfectionist. When she's ruling my mind, I'm always looking for the part of my life that doesn't look the way it's "supposed to be." Rather than focus on the parts of my life that are fantastic, she will focus all of her attention on the parts that aren't, and then convince me it's because I am not good enough unless it's perfect.

But when I use these emotions and behaviors to spot her thoughts, I no longer have to try to manipulate life so I don't feel a certain way. I can just let life happen. I can take risks, even if my Inner Critic tells me not to. I can make choices that might fail, but if they do, I can learn from the failure. I can handle the possibility of judgment or rejection because if I am judged or rejected, I don't listen to my IC tell me that means I am not good enough. I don't have to ward off anything. And that is exactly why I am living my passions and going for my dreams.

Is it uncomfortable? You bet it is! But I continually practice being comfortable with being uncomfortable. Whether you are listening to your IC or not, life is uncomfortable. I am going to be uncomfortable going for my dreams, and even more uncomfortable *not* going for my dreams. So, I would rather live a life going for my dreams. As Norman Vincent Peale said in his book *The Power of Positive Thinking,* "Shoot for the moon. Even if you miss, you'll land among the stars."

INDICATION SIGNS ON DISPLAY

Here are some personality traits and behaviors that may actually be Indication Signs. If you regularly experience these, your IC is likely sitting up high up on her throne.

Perfectionism

Perfectionism, the hallmark of Queen Perfectionist, shows up many different ways. In fact, many people who don't consider themselves to be perfectionists demonstrate perfectionist behaviors. I encourage you to get real with yourself and do a little inventory to see where you stand. Which of these ways of being is familiar to you?

- Having a difficult time accepting being "second best" in any endeavor
- Avoiding activities or tasks when you know that you won't be the best
- Giving up on a task instead of not doing it perfectly
- Sacrificing your own well-being to make something perfect
- Believe that there is a "right" and "wrong" way to do most things
- Sensitivity to rejection
- Obsessing about previous mistakes, mulling over what you did and did not do correctly
- Being a people pleaser
- Being judgmental and critical of others
- Feeling that no matter how good life is, it's not good enough – something's missing
- Believing that asking for help is a sign of weakness
- Needing to be in control
- Taking on extra work to make sure it gets done right

Being a perfectionist doesn't mean a perfect-looking life, nor even the desire for one. As I've said, I would never have considered myself a perfectionist – and yet I spent years trying to perfect my career, trying to perfect my body, and trying to get my husband and my kids to match the ideal pictures in my head in the belief that this was where my happiness lay. The unending theme song of my inner critic is that nothing is ever good enough. That's perfectionism.

When I am trying to reach my ideal perfect standard of some part of my life, my Indication Signs include anxiety, crankiness, and a desire to eat lots of ice cream. But my biggest Indication Sign is when I lapse into criticizing others. As soon as I start that, I know my Inner Critic is sitting up high on the throne in my mind.

Worry

Worry is a useless emotion, but your Inner Critic is convinced that being anxious is somehow being productive, as if that will control how your future will play out. Queen Guilt worries that others will be disappointed in or upset with you. Queen Wishy Washy worries that you can't make decisions for yourself – or that your choices will be disastrous. Queen Perfectionist worries about whatever you need to change or fix to make your life as perfect as possible.

Whichever Queen rules you, her unspoken message is that you are always in danger of something bad happening, and that worrying will prepare you for whatever danger lies ahead. But research indicates that eighty-five percent of what we worry about doesn't actually come about, and, of the things that actually do happen, seventy-nine percent is manageable. That means that ninety-seven percent of what you worry about could be only a product of your mind.

Worry is simply a repetitive negative thought pattern. Unfortunately, your body doesn't know that. Your body thinks you're in danger, which means you're flooded with the adrenaline and cortisol that are designed to help you run away from actual danger but, when left unchecked, can cause physical disease. Worry is an important Indication Sign that the IC's thoughts are running on a vicious loop in your mind.

Distraction

Most people spend much of their day in distraction without even realizing it. I do it too. The other night in bed, I pulled out my phone to look at my calendar, and the next thing I knew, I had been watching animal rescue videos for forty-five minutes!

Distraction is simply your mind's way of disconnecting when you feel anxious. Knowing that is the first step to becoming aware of this Indication Sign and choosing to do something else instead.

You can simply notice: When are you engaged in an activity without actively deciding to or wanting to? When are you checking out mentally and why? Is it around family? Friends? Co-workers? Don't judge these observations, simply be with them.

Your Indication Signs, observed without judgment, can be your greatest access to seeing your IC in action, to seeing clearly where your mind goes and when. You must be aware of the paths your mind likes to take before you can begin to question why or whether it helps or hurts you.

What people often find is that the more they remove themselves from distraction, the more they are forced to actually deal with a lot of the emotions they've been avoiding. This is uncomfortable, but it's the path to freedom.

Control

Many people have a fundamental belief that if they work hard, they can make things happen and get results. They're convinced that if they slow down and stop pushing so hard, their whole life and career might come crashing down.

The need for control pops up in several Queen Inner Critics. Queen Inadequate wants to control the outcome of even uncontrollable situations. Queen Victim and Queen Guilt want to control other people's thoughts so that they never judge you or are disappointed in you. In all these cases, the Inner Critic in question is focused on control, much like distraction, in order to ward off painful emotions. But the belief that we can control the direction of our future, what others think about us, and whether or not life matches our expectations is the very illusion that creates most of our pain and suffering. When we're blindly following our Inner Critic's attempts to control our life, we are not allowing life to be exactly as it is. Learning to let go of control is an essential aspect of personal growth, as well as of success and fulfillment.

When you can practice allowing your life to show up exactly as it is meant to and allow things to happen and materialize without trying to control, fix, manipulate, or dominate yourself, someone else, or events, you can begin to recognize that the very parts of life your IC has been trying to control are the parts you have never and will never have control over in the first place. Letting go of this control is what opens up space for true change and transformation.

Your IC will wholeheartedly resist this. Your IC wants to keep you working hard, running fast, and making sure that life fits your ideal picture of the way it should be. This is what I refer to as "shoulding on yourself." Your IC's belief is, "If it is to be, it is up to me." So no matter how much you do, how hard you work, how many goals you accomplish, you never feel fulfilled, and instead will create a chronic sense of lack, overwhelm, and exhaustion. This is because your IC is insatiable in its attempts to control everyone and everything so that you can feel good. But rather than feeling good, the attempt to control produces feelings of frustration, anger, worry, and overwhelm. These feelings and the behaviors they produce are your Indication Signs.

Author and thought leader Byron Katie says, "When you argue with reality, you lose – but only 100 percent of the time." Your IC's attempts to script the direction of reality sets you up to lose.

When you clearly see your Indication Signs that are connected to control, you can begin to tap into the immense power of allowing people, things, and situations to be as they are without judging them, trying to fix them, or wanting to change them. If your IC continues to try to control, you will never be able to find the true peace and fulfillment you crave. Action is important, but you also have to learn to balance it out with your ability to allow.

Seeking Pleasure
One of the ways the Inner Critic has trained us to feel better is to seek pleasure – a major Indication Sign.

We often don't understand the difference between joy and pleasure. The desire for pleasure drives our want for something external in our lives to make us feel a particular way. We could seek pleasure in the form of food, drinking, drugs, cigarettes, exercising, shopping, even goal-setting.

There is a lot of money made in our culture on the promises of pleasure. Our culture convinces us though movies, TV, magazines, advertisements, and social media that we should feel happiness all of the time. We're constantly bombarded with ways to feel pleasure: pleasure through eating, drinking, buying clothes, and spending money on gadgets or things. The promises of pleasure are everywhere. Drinking a Coke makes you smile. Driving a BMW makes you successful. Carrying a Louis Vuitton bag makes you sophisticated.

The pleasure we experience from all of these things produces dopamine hits to our brains. The result is that we seek more and more of the thing that brings us pleasure. And when we are convinced that we should feel only happiness all of the time, we seek out this pleasure as a way to avoid feeling emotions that we associate with pain. So no matter how much we eat, drink, work, or exercise in the pursuit of the dopamine hit, we need more and more of it to numb ourselves.

This is the false pleasure that your Inner Critic is conditioned to seek. Remember, your Inner Critic wants to shield you from pain. So your Inner Critic has convinced you that feeling your feelings is wa-a-ay too scary.

What would life be like if you stopped using pleasure to shield yourself from emotions that you consider too scary to feel? When your life is guided by the stories of your Inner Critic, there are a lot of painful emotions that are associated with those stories. And the way you have habitually coped with this pain is to find ways to escape the emotion.

But escaping the emotion doesn't mean that you are actually happier or having less of an experience of the emotion. It's just that in the moment, you're temporarily numb to the emotion. This is the fundamental difference between pleasure and joy. Pleasure is temporary. It is often what we seek externally from the world because it temporarily changes how we feel internally.

Lack of Confidence

When you lack confidence, you feel insecure about yourself and your abilities. You can't count on yourself to take the actions that will support the life you want to live. Instead, you allow your feelings to dictate the actions you are willing to take. Queen Perfectionist damages your self-esteem with her striving. Queen Bad Girl convinces you that you're hopelessly awful. Queen Inadequate reluctantly admits that you're trying – but it's useless, because nothing you do will ever be enough.

But confidence is built, not something you're born with. And the only way to do that, to cultivate confidence, is to be willing to take action even when the emotions that accompany that action are very uncomfortable.

Self-doubt comes from the thoughts in our minds. Failure, rejection, and inadequacy do not actually exist without thoughts. In order to feel that we've failed, been rejected, or are inadequate, we have to assign that meaning to an event or circumstance in our lives.

What you think of yourself is what either creates or diminishes self-confidence. Because confidence is a feeling. And since all of our feelings come from our thinking, it really boils down to examining the thoughts that are floating around in your mind. If your thoughts make you feel worthy, valued, strong, and capable, you will generate confidence, even in the face of failing at something, being rejected, or making a mistake. If your thoughts make you feel insecure, not good enough, and fearful, this will deplete your confidence because you believe those thoughts are true.

Most people do not feel confident in one or more areas of their lives. The reason for that is that they've been listening to their Inner Critic thoughts and mistaking them for facts. They're afraid to feel the painful emotions that come up, and so they've set life up to avoid any situations that would cause these emotions to surface.

46

Indecisiveness

Most people live their life by default, letting things happen to them instead of making conscious decisions and taking actions that are in alignment with the life they want to live. When we avoid making decisions, procrastinate, and take no actions, we are living from fear and scarcity, driven by Queen Wishy Washy, the Inner Critic whose inclination is to keep us safe rather than help us move forward.

It takes a huge amount of energy to stay spinning in indecision. When we have goals like losing weight, changing a job, getting married, or leaving a marriage, our Inner Critic holds us still, spending a lot of energy thinking about it, but taking no action unless there is a guarantee that life will go exactly as we want it to.

Your IC reconsiders the same decisions over and over because she's trying to find the ways in which you can avoid discomfort. This is, quite simply, why you don't have the life you want. Bullied into inaction by your IC, you stay in the swirl of not knowing, of believing that there are right and wrong decisions.

It may be that you don't know what you want – in part because you haven't made enough decisions to find out. Making choices allows you to risk experiencing what you don't want – which can only help clarify what you do. You don't need to know what you want before you make a decision to take any single action. You can simply take an action and see how it goes.

Deciding on an action frees up your energy. The decision itself is neutral – there is no right or wrong. Either way, you're going to move your life forward. No matter what happens from the decision, the lessons from it will continue to propel your life. Indecision arises from your old brain and its fear-based ideas of how to keep you safe.

Write down the decisions you have to make. Look at the energy it takes to consider these decisions every single day. Stop thinking about it. Make a decision of action and then honor that decision. You don't even have to be clear about the reason or the "why" behind the decision. When you decide something, you move forward in creating that future. Decide to either want what is or make a decision to take action to create something different. Live into that bigger decision and the delayed gratification as to how life is going to go once you've made this first decision.

FOLLOW THE INDICATION SIGNS TO RESET YOUR THINKING

Albert Einstein said that problems can't be solved with the same mindset that created them. Similarly, you can't make changes until you see how your IC's thoughts are creating the same feelings and causing you to take the same actions over and over. You have to be able to bear witness to the ways you have habitually thought for much of your life, ways you may not even be aware of, that are creating the same patterns in your life over and over.

Observing an emotional state like insecurity, anger, sadness, or fear allows you to *un-memorize* the old emotional state by becoming intimately familiar with the thoughts that led to that state. You need self-observation (self-awareness) to look at emotional states that have such a negative impact on your thoughts and behavior. The practice is to surrender that emotion to a better thought. And when you practice intentionally thinking different thoughts, you create separation between your old, conditioned, habitual mind and a newly rewired mind.

Becoming aware of your Indication Signs gives you the opportunity to step out of the old mind and into the new one by choosing a different thought, a different way of thinking that opens a door. All the old, expended energy that you used to spend living in your old emotional state will instead be channeled into getting conscious of the unconscious, conditioned Inner Critic mind.

This is when we begin to close the gap between the unconscious and the conscious. Investigating the Indication Signs elevates our consciousness.

As you Investigate the Indication Signs, it is important to remember that some emotions can be distractions from *other* emotions. Analyzing one emotion will always generate another emotion. You can then use your sadness, your anger, your resentment, or your anxiety to avoid taking different actions that give you different results. Because let's face it: sometimes transforming one's life can feel scarier than staying stuck!

This is where Gabrielle was for a *long* time. She couldn't face her own fear, so she remained stuck for years in sabotaging her entire life because that at least was familiar to her. She knew how to live a messed up, drug-addicted life. But she had no clue how to live a normal, happy life in which she was committed to building a career and a healthy relationship with herself and with other people.

It takes time to learn to become comfortable with being uncomfortable. Emotions like fear, sadness, anger, and resentment are powerful, especially if you've been suppressing your emotions for most of your life. Suddenly opening up to them will feel life-changing and incredibly profound, and requires both focus and effort.

But emotions, as you will eventually discover, don't necessarily mean anything. Emotions are only vibrations in your body. Feeling an uncomfortable emotion won't kill you. Avoiding it simply distracts you from taking different actions that could produce different results.

Self-awareness can be like peeling an onion – whatever you're thinking or feeling, there's always another layer underneath. The self-questioning involved in self-awareness can lead to this kind of endless spiral. Layer upon layer upon layer. And, in many cases, not only do deeper levels not provide you with anything useful, but the mere act of peeling them back can generate more thoughts that produce anxiety, stress, and self-judgment.

When you are willing to learn to feel *all* of your emotions, you can then change the trajectory of your life. You can feel the feelings, but take the actions that are in alignment with the life you really want to be living. You don't have to let your anxiety and fear of judgment, failure, or rejection stop you. As author Susan Jeffers says in her classic book *Feel the Fear and Do It Anyway,* "Every time you encounter something that forces you to 'handle it,' your self-esteem is raised considerably. You learn to trust that you will survive, no matter what happens. And in this way your fears are diminished immeasurably."

Self-awareness doesn't have an arrival point, a destination when you are "done," but the whole thing is wasted if it does not result in self-acceptance. Self-awareness can make you more miserable if it is coupled with self-judgment – then you're merely becoming more aware of all the ways you deserve to be judged.

Dethroning Your Inner Critic is about moment-by-moment awareness, about catching your IC in power over your mind and removing it from her control. Your mind can either be your greatest gift, or a dangerous place to be. Learning to spot your Indication Signs will tip you off next time you're distracting yourself from your feelings. Recognizing the feeling or behavior, and then getting curious about the thought, leads you to parts of your mind you may never have investigated before.

I have my automatic, conditioned ways of thinking that lead me to react in ways that I'm not proud of. We all do. I've come to terms with those flaws in myself, so I'm able to find forgiveness of those flaws within myself and in others.

WHAT ARE YOUR INDICATION SIGNS?

Your Inner Critic's Indication Signs have become so much a part of your inner environment that it's like the air you breathe. The thoughts and behaviors feel normal, and you don't question them. But your Inner Critic mind is always operating behind the scenes.

Indication Signs fall into these categories:
• Thoughts and mind chatter
• Automatic behaviors

- Body sensations
- Body language
- Tone of voice

Step One
Write Out a Comprehensive List of Your Indication Signs

The late Wayne Dyer said, "Don't just do something, stand there!" Take ten minutes to get quiet and still. Make a list of all the uncomfortable body sensations and unhealthy behaviors that frequently show up in your life.

Examples of behaviors:
- Lashing out in anger
- Wanting to isolate yourself
- Over-eating
- Under-eating
- Drinking alcohol excessively, engaging in drug use to numb out
- Road rage
- Complaining
- Blaming
- Judging
- Criticizing
- Over-exercising
- Over-working
- Over-scheduling/ keeping busy

Examples of body sensations
- Tightness in chest
- Headache
- Back or neck pain
- Tightness in neck or shoulders
- Stomachache
- Fatigue
- Low energy
- Lack of sex drive

Step Two
Ask Yourself, What Feeling Lies Underneath?

Learn how to feel your feelings and not resist them, not react to them, and not avoid them. The trick is to go from the extremes of either getting sucked into your IC's drama or avoiding her, to simply watching her. You may have been running away from pain for so long that you've never known who you really are when separated from your IC. When you have access to all of your emotions, it may feel like you are meeting a part of yourself for the first time. This is the only way that you can allow yourself to take actions that are in alignment with the life you want to design, even if that action will make you feel really uncomfortable.

Examples of Feelings
- Boredom
- Pessimism
- Frustration/Impatience
- Overwhelm
- Disappointment
- Doubt
- Worry
- Blame
- Discouragement
- Sadness
- Anger
- Resentment
- Jealousy
- Insecurity
- Guilt
- Shame
- Rage/Hatred
- Insecurity/Unworthiness
- Helplessness/Hopelessness/Despair

Step Three
Use the Feeling to Investigate What You're Thinking

Your thoughts are causing the feeling. Any thought you don't want to get past you unchecked requires investigation. Instead of wallowing in or getting lost in the feeling, focus your attention on the feeling and take a few minutes to write down the answers to these questions:

- What am I thinking when I feel this feeling?
- What do I say to myself and to others when I am feeling this way?
- How am I acting when I am feeling this way?
- What other emotions spring forth when I am feeling this way?
- What does this feeling feel like in my body?
- What circumstances trigger this feeling?
- What past memories have made this feeling surface?
- Is there a familiar theme to my thoughts that create this feeling?
- What other thoughts can I choose to have when I am feeling this feeling?
- What other reactions can I have when I am feeling this feeling?

Investigating your old habits of thoughts, feelings, and behaviors, reveals the *old* you that must be pruned away. You are dismantling your old circuits. Your memories can now be stored as wisdom and opportunities to learn about what has made you, *you*. When Michelangelo was asked how he sculpted the famous statue of David, he replied that he chipped away at all that wasn't David. When you Investigate Your Indication Signs, you are chipping away at all of your old thoughts, feelings, and behaviors to reveal the best version of yourself.

CHAPTER SIX

n

NEUTRALIZE THE
NEVER-ENDING MESSAGES

The beginnings of your sense of yourself start to take shape when you are about three or four years old – and that sense of self that was formed all those years ago is still what runs you today. That's pretty scary when you think about it!

Your young self started to form opinions about how important you are, how loved you are, whether you are smart enough, and how much you matter to others. These beliefs become a solid part of your sense of self, and they continue to play a huge role in almost every aspect of your life, from your self-esteem to the people with whom you choose to be in relationships.

The existence of the Inner Critic is hard-wired into our DNA and stems from the human instinct to avoid pain and situations that can cause us harm. Back when we were cave men and women, we needed this instinct to protect us. We needed to make sure that we weren't going to be eaten by tigers. We also needed to make sure that the tribe accepted us, otherwise we died. Period.

In modern life, you no longer have to worry about tigers. Instead, emotional pain and vulnerability are your enemies. Your

Inner Critic seeks to keep you safe from the pain of being hurt or rejected, of failing, being criticized, disappointed, shamed, or embarrassed.

We put all our focus on our outer environment for our sense of ourselves. We believe that changes in our outer environment will lead to changes in how we feel inside. This is the way many people live their lives, with attachments and demands that the world around them is a match for who their IC says they *should* be. If you just become the ideal version of you, the Inner Critic affirms, then you will never again have to worry about being hurt.

How does this play out in your life? There are two possible scenarios:

A) You walk into a party where you know no one. To protect you, your Inner Critic pipes up: "You better go stand in the corner over there, because why would anyone want to talk to *you?*" So you go stand in the corner, and you don't get to know any of the other guests. The next week, you find out that some of those same people grabbed coffee together and didn't invite you. Your Inner Critic – in this case, Queen Inadequate – says, "See, it really is *true* that people just don't find you interesting."

B) At the same party, the Queen Perfectionist variant of your Inner Critic warns: "You better go in there and make sure you're the life of the party! Otherwise, no one will be interested in you." By the end of the night, you're exhausted from the effort of trying to be universally liked.

Your IC is either the scaredy-cat voice holding you back or the perfectionistic one pushing you to go for broke. Either way, you have been to a party under the spell of an Inner Critic who isn't really you. She is a part of your inner life, but not the one that you should allow to be in charge.

If that's true, then what the heck is she doing there?

Your mind is constantly speaking to you, and has been for forever, trying to get everything in your life to be the way it is supposed to, or you are *not okay*. And in case you haven't noticed, although you have had a lot of things in your life go the way you want, you are still not okay. This is because your mind is the biggest bully on the planet!

But it doesn't have to be this way. Though you can't silence your mind, you can direct your mind, much like you steer a car in the direction you want it to go. Neutralizing the Never-ending Messages is an important step in doing just that.

When you know how to direct your mind, you feed and nurture yourself from the inside. You stop feeling like you're in a constant state of needing something outside yourself to be different in order to feel good. You stop needing someone else to make you feel loved, or more money to make you feel secure or successful. You stop looking for a better external environment to feel better. You stop using your mind for complaining and judging.

Instead, see your mind as separate from you. You can recognize, maybe for the first time, that you have a lot of stored up feelings from your past, and your mind continually reflects all of your stored up emotions back to you. When you take the time to look underneath, and look deeper, you will see all of the beliefs that you have stored from your past. That is what blocks your ability to feel whole.

This chapter is about learning how to release those old IC beliefs so that you can stop trying to control the outside world to make sure nothing and no one taps into your stored-up pain. When you know how to use your mind to release the energy that is blocking you, rather than trying to manipulate the world outside, you return to feeling whole.

Imagine a life where you stop protecting yourself by trying to control all the people and the things that bother you. When you let go of what's blocking you and feel whole on the inside, this is what changes the trajectory of your life. When more people understand that it is never the outside world that causes our problems, this is when our world can become so much calmer.

THE QUEEN'S ENGLISH

When you Neutralize the Never-ending Messages of your Inner Critic, it allows you to recognize where her story from your past continues to show up every time you're upset. When you see your inner disturbance is really about what she's been saying to you over and over on endless loop for your whole life, you can learn how to use your past to rewire your mind and create a different future for yourself.

Remember that the only place your past actually exists is in your mind. The past is over.

The future you are designing is also only in your mind. The only thing that you actually have control over is this very moment. And what exists in this moment is the thoughts that you are thinking *right now*.

This is where the tools of Dethroning Your Inner Critic can be life-changing. Because it is not your past that causes you pain. There are the facts about what happened in the past, and then there's your Inner Critic's story about what happened. And this is a *huge* distinction. Your past as it exists right now is only your Inner Critic's story about your past. When you are asked by someone to recount what happened when you were a child, or a young adult, the details that you would recount would be your Inner Critic's version of the story. She has assigned a lot of meaning to the events of your past based on her Never-Ending Message. That meaning she assigned is what's been causing so much of your suffering.

It's not the events themselves. It's what she says the events *mean* about you. About your life. About your worth. About your ability to love yourself and allow others to love you. Your feelings are never created by what happened. Your feelings arise when you believe your (her) thoughts about what happened.

All of this means that whatever pain you carry inside you was and is formed by your Inner Critic's version of the story of your past – whether that past was fifteen years ago, or fifteen minutes. Your feelings that you had at age three, ten, seventeen, twenty-five, and even this morning were all formed by the automatic thoughts of your Inner Critic. If your IC is now repeating the same Never-ending Messages that you had at age eight, then you will experience the same feeling that you did then. When you experience pain from events of your past, what you're really experiencing is listening to the thoughts of your Inner Critic and mistaking them for the truth.

Many of the thousands of clients I have seen in my professional career have experienced horrible circumstances. Abuse, neglect, abandonment. And when they experienced these circumstances, their automatic mind formed a lot of thoughts and beliefs. But the good news is that the only way you can continue to experience pain from that circumstance is if you continue to assign *the same thought and belief* to the circumstance.

Let's slow this down because it's important. If you allow yourself to continue to believe the old thoughts and beliefs about the circumstances of your past, then you are continuing to feel victimized by those circumstances. You are continuing to feel the shame associated with the circumstances. You are continuing to allow your Inner Critic to cause you pain about what happened. In essence, *you* are continuing to cause yourself pain. Because you can't experience pain from your past unless you are thinking thoughts right now that cause you pain.

Sought-after motivational speaker Les Brown tells the story of being labeled "educable mentally retarded" and being moved back from fifth grade to fourth. He failed his eighth grade level as well. But in high school, his speech and drama teacher, LeRoy Washington, changed his life by telling him, "Someone's opinion of you does not have to become your reality."

You, like Les Brown, have a choice about how you want to think. When you practice the tools of Dethroning Your Inner Critic and prevent her from ruling your mind, you get to choose the thoughts you are going to think about the events in your life.

CORE BELIEF:
YOU OR YOUR INNER CRITIC?

We have a part of our brain called the Reticular Activating System (RAS) that is the gatekeeper of the information we pay attention to. When you buy a new car, for example, you may find that suddenly all you see on the road around you is the same make and model. That's because your RAS has filtered what you notice.

Why is it that you can't remember what you had for breakfast two days ago, but you can remember where you were standing on the playground in fifth grade when Susie said she no longer wanted to be your friend? When we experience emotion that causes us pain, our brain wants to figure out how to avoid feeling this pain in the future. This is where your IC swoops in to save you by declaring something like, "There must be something wrong with me for Susie to decide to stop being my friend. I better not let anyone get too close to me again, or they will reject me."

This is how your IC's thoughts get reinforced. "Something's wrong" is the Never-Ending Message that can sabotage you and your life. In an effort to protect you, your IC creates the same repetitive messages that make you think something might go wrong, even when things are fine.

It's imperative to realize that all of your personal thoughts and beliefs exist only in your own inner world. They are not what everyone else thinks about you, and they do not even exist in the external world. See, you really have no idea why Susie stopped being your friend. But like most of us, you live as though every thought you have about yourself is an absolute fact.

This is the RAS at work: you give attention and focus to that which allies with your belief systems. As author Don Miguel Ruiz wrote, "We only see what we want to see; we hear what we want to hear. Our belief system is just like a mirror that only shows us what we believe."

When we see what we want to see and hear what we want to hear, we create and live lives based on our/our Inner Critic's interpretation of the past. We see ourselves, our circumstances, and our relationships through the filters of our/her beliefs, most of which were formed when we were too young to understand mental discernment.

Core Belief

Every human being has a Core Belief about themselves. No matter what our past experiences have been, this is what we *all* have in common.

It begins with our family. All families have what psychology calls family dynamics – how members interact with each other. At a young age – three or four – we start observing those family dynamics to try to understand what makes us loved and valued by the people who matter most to us, and how we belong in the world. We get frightened if mommy or daddy gets upset or angry. When our brother or sister teases us, our feelings get hurt. Without realizing it, we internalize these experiences as, "Uh-oh, I'm bad," or, "I'm not loved," or, "Something is wrong with me." In other words, "I am not okay."

This is the beginning of our Core Belief about ourselves and how it first gets planted in our mind as some kind of objective truth. And this is how our Inner Critic mind gets formed. There is a defining moment in which we feel the initial pain. That becomes a suppressed hurt inside of us, and we try to find a way to make sure that we never experience that pain again. So, our mind tries to manage aspects of our lives to ensure this. How? Our Inner Critic spends the rest of our lives pointing out everything that we need to fix, perfect, or change to avoid being hurt ever again.

The problem is that everything she tries to make us do to avoid this hurt actually creates more of it. If we are running from failure, failure – in some way, shape, or form – keeps showing up. If we're running from feeling unimportant, we continue to have experiences that undermine our value.

The IC doesn't just advocate that we run away from what we fear. She also wants us to run toward what we crave. When she says we are unlovable, she tells us we need the whole family to prove their love. When she says we "need" something outside ourselves to feel happy, she urges us to chase whatever it is in order to heal the hurt from our core issue.

Our IC mind views anything that might trigger us into that suppressed pain as a threat, and switches into automatic and conditioned ways of dealing with that trigger. When we are threatened, our brain goes into fight-or-flight mode. We fight it by trying to control a part of our life so we don't get triggered, or we resist the problem entirely by avoiding doing anything differently in that area of our life. We operate in this automatic way that our IC has created, which makes everything much worse.

I worked with a highly paid VP of a healthcare company who knew she was meant to do something different. She had spent years of her life in overwhelm, stress, and dissatisfaction. Once she began to practice the tools of DYIC, she clearly saw that she'd been avoiding the fear and uncertainty of starting a new career, even though empowering young women in the corporate world was her passion. She was afraid her husband and children would be disappointed in her if she left a big career to follow her dreams. She was afraid of disappointing her boss and all the employees she managed. She had spent her childhood not wanting to disappoint her father, and then continued this pattern as an adult. Once she saw this, she realized she was more afraid of others' disappointment than she was of failing to fulfill her dreams.

Different people get upset over different things because we all have different things that trigger us into our Core Belief. If you look at your life, you may begin to see that the same trigger shows up over and over and over. It may be triggered by your child, your spouse, your boss, your mom, or your friend, but it is the same core pain that gets repeatedly triggered. This is actually your Core Belief, popping up over and over. The resulting IC's habitual mind chatter keeps reinforcing that Core Belief, and creating untold suffering in your life.

The people, circumstances, and things in your life that cause you to struggle are all mirrors of your IC screaming her Never-ending Messages. When your boss criticizes the way you handled the meeting, for example, it drives you crazy. It keeps you up at night with thoughts like, "If she really knew how much value I provide for this company, she would never have said the things she did!" Her comments leave you feeling frustrated, angry, overwhelmed, and anxious – but it isn't about your boss.

Consider for a moment that all of these feelings are actually your IC's Never-ending Message at play. Is it possible that what's most important to your IC in this scenario is that your boss values you? Is it possible that when you feel that someone is judging or criticizing you, it makes you feel that this person doesn't value you? Is it also possible that you've felt this feeling before? In fact, is it possible that whenever you're most upset, angry, or overwhelmed, what's really stirring you up is the thought that someone is in some way judging you or thinking less of you?

When you learn to spot this Never-Ending Message, you have the power to see your IC's thoughts as nothing more than computer-like programming. Becoming the observer of the message makes the space to change the internal focus of your mind and elevate your internal energy, rather than allowing the same broken-record message to deplete your internal energy.

Although the circumstances might appear to be different, the underlying message remains the same. And the underlying message is what your IC is most trying to protect you from. In other words, your IC's one and only job has been to figure out how to prevent you from feeling emotional pain. Your IC rationalizes that if you can find a way to control what others think of you, you will find the freedom and peace you crave. So your IC has you running in circles and trying to be valued, liked, and respected so you look like you have it all together.

Which is exactly why no matter how much you are valued, liked, and respected, you *still* don't have the peace, joy, and contentment you crave.

Hearing and seeing your Never-Ending Message is about waking up to the hamster wheel that you've unconsciously been on. When you see that your whole life has been spent trying to figure out how to avoid pain, you are then free. The freedom is about seeing the Never-ending Message for what it is: nothing more than your IC's computer programing at work. When you know how to spot it, you can then step away from it. You can unhook from her message.

My IC's Never-Ending Message to me is that I am less than. When my son is making choices I don't agree with, my Queen Perfectionist IC chimes in: "What if he fails? What if he remains unhappy? What do I need to do as his mom to get his life to turn out? Because if his life turns out, if he is happy and successful and fulfilled, that would mean I did a good job – *I wasn't less than as a mom.*"

If a business decision doesn't pan out the way I'd hoped, my IC chimes in again: "That's because you aren't a good enough businesswoman. If you were more organized, this wouldn't have happened." Again, Queen Perfectionist has me comparing myself to the most savvy businesswomen I know. If I'm not like that, she says, I'm not good enough.

No matter the circumstance, my IC will assign the same meaning over and over. But her meaning is just that – *the meaning that* she *assigns.* There is no truth in the thought, "If my son isn't happy, I wasn't a good enough mom," or, "If my business decision didn't turn out as planned, I am not as good of a business person as someone else."

When I can see my IC's machinery, I can unhook. I can direct my mind away from her fabricated story, and steer my mind toward the facts: My son's happiness is his responsibility. My responsibility is to love him, and that is all I can do. Sometimes my business decisions will turn out – and sometimes they won't. I will make the best decision I know how to make in the moment, and I will learn from the outcome.

The good news is that you, like me, can recognize your IC's

Never-Ending Message, identify the negative Core Belief at the heart of it all, and begin the practice of interrupting this cycle.

To find your Core Belief, look to see where you have felt somehow "not okay" in your life. You're searching for thoughts and feelings that are familiar to you, and in some way are repetitive. As you consider this, remember, the Core Belief is not the truth. It's the automatic meaning your IC assigns to the circumstances of your life.

Bringing awareness to your Core Belief can feel very uncomfortable, especially if you've been making it true for much of your life. I call that "truthifying." Instead of continuing to avoid feeling it, we need to turn toward it and face it. By facing it, we can begin to separate ourselves from our IC. Can you see that your Core Belief is an illusion that was created by your Inner Critic a very long time ago? This realization is what makes your IC lose her hold over you. This is the start of reinventing the way you experience yourself in your life.

In order to understand your Core Belief, you need to be willing to look at your past. You need to be willing to see where your IC is keeping you stuck by assigning meaning that causes you to drag the weight of your emotional pain with you throughout your life. You have to be willing to retell the story of your past from a new, rewired mind. You have to be willing to ask yourself, "Why have I been dragging this story around with me for my whole life? Is it serving a purpose for me?"

HOW TO IDENTIFY YOUR CORE BELIEF

Make some space in your day to go back in time. Block out a time when you are alone and can really reflect on your memories. Remember a specific event in your childhood where you felt emotional pain. Allow yourself to go back and put yourself in the emotion of what happened. Now take some time to answer these questions:

1. What's the belief you took on as a result of this event?
2. What are the *facts* of what happened? If you were a fly on the wall, could you see it? Try to leave out any details that a fly on the wall couldn't see. This can help you separate the facts from the automatic interpretations of your IC.
3. What was the interpretation, or meaning, that you assigned to those facts? What did you make it mean about you? About someone else? About your life?
4. Can you identify other times in your life where you experienced being triggered this way? What was the interpretation or meaning that was assigned to those circumstances?
5. List some other major upsets that you have had in your life, and examine whether your Core Belief was at play in those upsets. We are trying to identify a pattern – your IC's repetitive message. She assigns that same meaning to the times when you're most upset. This is the fundamental belief that runs your life.
6. Who you are blaming in your life? Blame is a way your Inner Critic distracts you from the pain of your Core Belief.
   • What are you blaming people and circumstances for?
   • How is that protecting you from being intimate with your own thoughts and feelings?
7. What are you are most trying to prove? Here's an example. Consider that your IC's Core Belief is that you're unimportant. As a result of this belief, you unconsciously take on relationships and projects that reinforce this view of yourself. You are constantly trying to prove that you're important, that you have value. Much of your energy goes toward trying to escape the feeling that you are unworthy.
8. What are your biggest fears? Make a list of your fears. Fear is FALSE EVIDENCE APPEARING REAL. When we experience fear, we are avoiding something that we are afraid will trigger us into our Core Belief.
9. What are the characteristics of your own parents that make you uncomfortable? How is this connected to your Core Belief about yourself?

10. What shows up in some of your most challenging relationships that trigger your Core Belief about yourself?

My client Karen believed she was unlovable because her mother, in a fit of rage, told her that she would never be as good as her brother when she was six years old. Karen spent the rest of her life trying to be pretty, smart, athletic, and successful – she, like me, was listening to Queen Perfectionist. She struggled with bouts of bulimia to keep her weight under control. She felt like she had to maintain an image of success and accomplishment in order for other people to love and accept her.

As a young adult, she had many friends, but none with whom she felt truly connected. She wouldn't ever reveal her insecurities to anyone, because she believed that she could never let anyone know that she wasn't good enough. She kept this shame to herself, and her Inner Critic kept her safe by pointing out all of her flaws and inadequacies, to ensure that she was always aiming for perfection.

By the time Karen and I began our work together, she had worked her way up professionally to become a CEO of a human resources management firm, and was burnt out both personally and professionally. Her relationship with her husband was more like that of a roommate. She blamed her feelings of anger on her boss for not valuing her contributions to the company, and on her husband for not being as successful as she and therefore putting all of the pressure on her to provide for their family.

Karen's breakthrough came when she was able to confront the Never-ending Message that her IC had perpetuated for almost her entire life: that she was worthless. Karen's IC needed her to perpetuate a vicious cycle of always needing to prove herself. She was reliving the pain from her childhood over and over in her present, by believing that her worthiness came from outside herself.

As hard as it was for her, Karen began to take responsibility for her automatic thoughts that perpetuated resentment and blame in her marriage and career. She learned to stop giving power to her mother's words. She changed her beliefs about the initial event when she was six, recognizing that her mother was parenting from a brokenness that she herself had developed in her own childhood. She stopped believing the conditioned thoughts that her Inner Critic had been playing on a loop for her whole life; these thoughts told her she was unlovable. She started to notice the blame and resentment she had built up in her marriage because she'd looked to her husband to give her worthiness that she hadn't learned to give to herself.

Karen is learning to ignore her Inner Critic's Never-Ending Message of her Core Belief. And thus, she is free.

Like Karen, all of your pain starts with your own Core Belief. It's not your boss, your husband, your mother-in-law, your aunt Betsy, your disrespect from your children, your thirty pounds you need to lose, or that you haven't met your company's projected goal for the month. People, circumstances, things – they all are what they are. People act the way they do because of their own inner thoughts, that lead to their inner emotions, that lead to their actions. Judgment, criticism, and disrespect toward others stems from judgment, criticism, and disrespect from within.

Most people don't take responsibility for their own thoughts. They spend their lives seeking fulfillment and happiness by controlling and manipulating everything outside themselves. When you see and hear the Never-ending Message about your Core Belief and can spot your IC assigning this belief to the people, events, and things that cause you to feel inwardly disturbed, you have found the true key to your happiness: everything begins in your mind.

When you change your thoughts, you change your life. This following list of questions is meant as a guide to help you tap into the Never-Ending Message that you've been receiving from your IC for your whole life. You will know that you've found it when you can't remember a time in your life when this feeling didn't exist.

Step One
Ask Yourself the Following Questions
1. What feelings make me most uncomfortable?
2. What is the most painful thing someone else could think of me?
3. What emotion do I try to protect myself from feeling?
4. What is my biggest fear?
5. What am I trying most to control in my life?
6. When have I been held back or stuck because of fear and doubt?
7. Is there something in my life I want right now, but I am stopped by fear?
8. What circumstances make me feel the most shame?

Step Two
Give Your Inner Critic a Name that Fits

Part of Neutralizing the Never-ending Messages is defusing your Inner Critic's power over you. And a great way to do that is to give her a nickname that helps you see who her for who she really is, which is, most importantly, *not you.*

My IC's name is Worrying Wilhelmina. Her Core Belief is that I am never good enough, and so her one of her favorite pastimes is to take me future-tripping. She's always trying to predict and control how my future will go because if she can control it, I will fulfill all of her expectations and demands, and then will finally feel good enough. Wilhelmina, it's clear, is also Queen Perfectionist.

When Wilhelmina is in control of my mind, she creates worry just by having me focused on a future arrival point. Once I get there, wherever "there" is, then I will be happy. Wilhelmina has made me feel this way since I was a little girl, and continues to show up on a daily basis. She says I am not a good enough mom when my kids don't make the choices I want them to. She says my husband isn't good enough when he is more quiet than I want him to be. She says I am not powerful enough when I am afraid

69

that I will never reach my big life visions. She is showing up even as I write this book.

I take Wilhelmina off the throne in my mind every single day. If I didn't, she would be taking me down some pretty nasty roads in my relationships and in my business. If I let her, she would rob me of the gratitude I have for my big, messy life. She would knock me out of peace, joy, and contentment and keep me rooted in fear and inadequacy.

I will be on this journey to dethrone her for the rest of my life, and I will never stop taking actions that are in alignment with a bigger version of myself and my life than she would ever have me believe is possible. I use the tools of DYIC every day to decipher the facts from her made-up story. If I didn't, I wouldn't have this life. I wouldn't be my big, bold, perfectly imperfect self.

If Wilhelmina had her way, I would hide my vulnerability and my faults. I wouldn't admit to days where I feel like a fraud, where my IC has swallowed me whole and I am swimming in my own shame. Days where I can't find my self-compassion, and I am convinced that I really am broken.

But then I remember. Then I wake up. "Oh, that's Wilhelmina." When I am separate from her, I can breathe again. I can let go. I can let myself be me, and let life go exactly where it is meant to go. I remember that life is like a river, and I can flow where the water takes me. I remember that when the water is choppy, it will once again be calm, as long as I surrender and flow.

What is your Inner Critic's name? Calling her by it is a big step toward recognizing when your IC is at it again, perpetuating her Never-ending Message.

Step Three
Rewrite the Story of Your Past

Neutralizing the Never-ending Messages means telling a different story than your Inner Critic's tired old favorites. You can heal anything that you feel has persisted from your past by rewriting your narrative. You can even transform your relationship with failure.

In this step, rewrite the story of your past from the perspective of your Authentic Self, not your Inner Critic. Change the story from being about your IC's Core Belief to the actual facts of the circumstances. Even if you have experienced horrible events like child abuse or neglect, the suffering that continues today is because the story about what happened was from the perspective of your IC. The way your IC stored these memories is different from how your Authentic Self would describe them. Rewriting your history heals your life.

Exercise One
Write a letter to your past self, recalling a painful event you experienced. What do you want your past self to know? What advice could you give to your past self? Find the places where you carry guilt, shame, or regret and re-tell the story of what happened using just the facts: "He said this. I did that. I cried." Notice how you feel, both when you're listening to your IC tell the story and also when you're the one retelling it. What thoughts do you want to hold onto regarding this story that are powerful and strengthening? What thoughts are you choosing to let go of?

Exercise Two
Write down all of your regrets, shame, and guilt that you carry from the past. Let it flow out of you onto the paper. Then, take this paper to a safe receptacle, light a match, and burn it. Release it back to the past, where it belongs!

Exercise Three
Think about a time when someone hurt you in the past, and consider telling the story from their perspective. What might they have been thinking when they did what they did? Can you imagine the pain their IC was causing them when they did what they did? This does not justify their behavior, but it helps to understand that it was their pain that caused them to feel what they felt, which caused their actions.

Neutralizing the Never-ending Messages by coming up with new thoughts on purpose allows you to put the past back in the past, and generate different actions. This *all* significantly reduces the likelihood of staying stuck in old, repetitive IC patterns of self-judgment and shame for the times when you weren't being who you are committed to be. You can choose to think kinder thoughts about yourself, no matter what the circumstances. Remember, we are all doing the best we can in the moment, based on what our thoughts and feelings are at the time. That includes you.

CHAPTER SEVEN

DESIGN YOUR LIFE

Act as if everything you desire is already here ...
treat yourself as if you already are what you'd like to become.
WAYNE DYER

Designing Your Life rewires your brain, creating a new mind with which to shape your life: a mind in which you are able to end the self-sabotage, and instead nurture positive feelings now instead of waiting for the circumstances of your life to be just right.

Most people don't realize that what you give attention to expands. When you learn to give attention to the thoughts created from your new mind instead of those of your Inner Critic, your life becomes more expansive. Living a purposeful life requires having purposeful thoughts. When you direct your mind toward your vision, your mind has the power to create anything.

First, you must make a commitment to the outcome you want. Once you make the commitment, stretch courageously into the actions that are in alignment with that future. Don't wait for full confidence before you take action. That won't come until later. You only need the courage necessary to face your Inner Critic's fear. You don't even need to know the "right" actions to take. Action taken from a place of already feeling whole is transformational.

This is what ends the vicious cycle.

You probably operated under the belief that creating positive change within yourself comes from changing your circumstances: making more money, having better relationships. The power is in seeing that it's the other way around. Consciously choosing thoughts like, "I feel blessed about the love I have in my life," or, "I am grateful for the life I have created," frees you from your Inner Critic's drama and creates space for living the life you want.

The M.I.N.D. Method supports my clients in moving from the unconscious, automatic habits of worry, blame, criticism, fixing, changing and perfecting, hiding feelings, and not speaking their truths, into a conscious choice to expand their capacity for abundance, love, and joy. They know that when you cultivate your goals from this place of freedom and abundance, rather than scarcity and brokenness, your entire life opens up to you.

This chapter has far more steps to it than preceding chapters, for the simple reason that Design Your Life is *about* taking steps – steps that will help you shape your life as you always hoped it would be.

Step One
Design Your Future

Without a clear vision for our lives, we are susceptible to allowing other people, and external circumstances, to steer us – and often in directions we don't want to go. That's why creating a compelling vision of the life you want is one of the most effective strategies for achieving that life. You can then use your vision like a compass to guide you to take the actions and make the choices consistent with turning the future you've imagined into reality.

A fulfilling and satisfying life doesn't happen by chance, but by design. It's designed from what you *want*, not what you don't. Many of us are much more comfortable with focusing on what we don't want. But this does not inspire action. Focusing on what you *do* want opens the opportunity to look at which actions you need to take to make your dreams come true.

First, focus on the result – the what, rather than the how. When you plan your life from your vision of the end result, it's easier to see a plan of action that will get you where you want to go. Think about the first step along the path to reach your vision. What action is the next step along your journey? See the gap between where you are and where you want to be. Fill in the gap with actions, one step at time.

Your actions will always take you somewhere other than where you are. Even if they don't lead you to the exact result you thought they would, they will *always lead somewhere.* If you stay in action and allow each outcome to help you learn and grow, the journey will be filled with excitement and possibility.

It's worth noting that actions don't produce results in a linear path. In fact, most people who have reached their goals describe a windy road with tons of unexpected twists and turns along the way. Your IC will call those twists and turns failures and inadequacies, and might try to convince you to give up. This is where your Reticular Activating System (RAS) is your friend.

Remember, the RAS is a part of your brain that acts like a filter, allowing certain things in and keeping others out. Visualizing the future you're designing helps train your RAS to help you. The more you visualize your goals and your desired outcome, the greater your chance of reaching them, because you're training your brain to focus on your goals and the path toward them. Clearly defining your goals sends your brain the signal that something is important and meaningful, so your RAS will begin to focus on it. Over time, your brain will pick up on the signs and clues that are in alignment with your vision.

Many people talk about wanting their lives to change without a specific picture in their mind about what will be different. Or, if they do have a clear picture, they don't visualize it as though they already have what they want right now.

This is key: *You have to train your brain to see yourself and your life as though these changes already exist.* If you want to love yourself, for example, it's imperative that you create a future vision in which you can clearly picture yourself already loving yourself and what is different about your life as a result.

When you love yourself, what will you be doing in your free time? What will your relationship with your partner look like? What boundaries will you be setting? What specific actions will you be doing in caring for your physical wellbeing, like eating, exercising, and sleeping? Will you be ending certain relationships that are unhealthy?

When you start to design a vision for how you want your life to go, you are creating a clear picture of your life in which you see yourself already there. You will actually *see* yourself already experiencing the feelings you're longing to feel, like joy, freedom, or gratitude. You can picture yourself standing taller, speaking up at work, feeling confident in yourself and your capabilities. When you create a vision for yourself and act as if that vision is here now, you are training your brain to create different filters.

Remember, your IC likes to focus on worst-case scenarios to protect you from any danger of them actually happening. But when your IC is whipping you back and forth from focusing on past mistakes and feelings of shame to fantasies about rejection and failure, you are at her mercy. She's controlling your emotions.

The problem with that is that when your IC is in control, your brain doesn't know the difference between her imagined ideas of what happened in the past and what it meant about you, and her fear of what might happen in the future and what it will mean about you. Remember, it is never what actually happened or what will happen that creates our emotions. It is the meaning that our IC assigns to the circumstances.

When you allow yourself to indulge in imagining your Inner Critic's worst-case scenarios, your brain operates as if those worst-case scenarios are already occurring. This is why, when you have to speak up in a work meeting, your heart is racing and your palms are sweaty before you even say a word. Without you realizing it, your IC has created the thought that you're going to sound stupid or that you'll be judged in some way, and your brain responds as though this is really happening.

When you create a vision, your brain will respond as though that vision has already occurred. So if you can visualize speaking up at that meeting with confidence and poise, you'll change the filter through which you see yourself and your life. And the more that you create this vision, the better you will actually be at building the ability to speak up at that meeting. Or talk to people who you don't know. Or show the love to your partner that will change the quality of your relationship.

When you design your life from the future, you are shifting your mind from the old stories of your Inner Critic to new thoughts that you think on purpose. This is how you create a new future. Creating a new future takes intention, effort, and creativity. You have to be willing to first observe your IC in the autopilot thinking that she has been spewing forever. Because, as I have said before, you can't change what you can't even see. This definitely requires more energy than staying on autopilot. But it makes all the difference between an ordinary life and an extraordinary life.

When you dethrone your Inner Critic, you rewire your hardwiring. You no longer allow yourself and your life to be defined by the story. Dethroning Your Inner Critic allows you to create your life from your future instead of your past. This means that the thoughts you are thinking about your future are new. You've never thought about yourself and your life in this way before. So these new thoughts create new feelings, which motivate you to take new actions.

It all starts with your thoughts. Either your thoughts are controlled by your Inner Critic or they are controlled by *you*. You get to decide. Remember, your thoughts create your reality, not the other way around. So if you take new actions over and over and over, you create a whole new life.

Ask yourself this question: "Do I want my Inner Critic to rule my future, or do I want to reinvent a new future?" In designing your future from this new place, you will create a completely different experience of yourself and your life. This is the power of practicing Dethroning Your Inner Critic on a daily basis. When you get your past out of your future, your future becomes a wide-open canvas to create whatever you want it to be.

When you are intentionally directing your mind to think new thoughts about yourself and your life, you can practice feeling happy and whole because you are no longer relying on the external world to define you. You can actually feel elevated emotions because they are unconditional. They are not dependent on external circumstances. The gap has closed, and no one or no event can make you feel anything you don't want to. You no longer want things in your life in order to fill your habitual state of lack or unworthiness.

I recommend declaring your future in a very specific way:

1. Get clear on what the future looks and feels like. The goal is to paint a picture that inspires you, stretches you, and leaves you feeling both giddy with excitement and a bit scared. Look at your whole life, as well as your relationships with yourself, with others including your significant other and children, who you are as a mother, who you are as a woman, who you are professionally.

2. Write your declared future in the present tense: "I am now ..." This makes you accountable for declaring your future in the here and now, not when you get around to it. I want you to have no choice but to design your future *now* and act accordingly starting *now*.

3. Bring self-compassion and tell the truth. Focus on what you want, not what you don't want. If you notice you're taking shots at yourself and others, try again. Tell the truth. If you can't tell say what you want with clarity and honesty, how can you get it?

This exercise can be confronting, so please remember that it is intended to measure where you are now vs where you want to be. It reveals which areas in your life are actually working and which aren't. Undertaken without judgment, it will bring clarity to where you are right now in comparison to where you want to be so that you can begin the journey to get there.

The first draft often asks to be rewritten in a more aspirational and possibility-oriented direction. Our first go at this exercise is often set up to have us get out of doing things that we might possibly fail at or be uncomfortable doing. Typically, we can't see this ourselves. A big clue that you could take another crack at writing your desired future is the use of the conditional tense "would be" ("I would be less critical"), pointing to the problems that need to be fixed rather than coming from inspiration.

When you create your life from the future, you step into a new possibility for who you know yourself to be. Living from this new place of possibility begins with enrolling yourself in your vision and really believing it. Then, enroll those around you in the belief that you will be living your life from this new place instead of the old way of living life from the story of who your IC says that you are.

When you are truly committed to living your life from a new possibility that is designed from your future, the old constraints imposed by your IC's view of you and your life begin to disappear. It takes ongoing practice, continually developing the muscle to see the new possibility that you have invented for yourself. This is why I encourage you to read and say your declared future daily and practice talking about it with people close to you. However, sometimes family and friends may be sarcastic and/or pessimistic about what you've declared – and you may be feeling some of that, too. When you're ready to share your future with them and you feel nervous and maybe a little embarrassed, tell them that. From vulnerability and courage, tell them that you simply want to share what you've created with them, not get their advice.

Please know that every day, you will be presented with opportunities to either live as if it's business as usual, your old IC way of living, or to come from a place beyond who you've been, what you've imagined, and what you experience as reality when your IC is on her throne.

To give you a feel for how this works, here's an example from one of my clients:

Designed Future, First Draft

My body is the healthiest it's ever been. I am finally able to say no to late-night snacking. I am free of stress eating after a day of "being good." I no longer feel the need to reward myself with sweets at the end of the day. I don't wake up feeling angry at myself for not having had willpower yet again. I like the way my body looks and feels and I like the sense of pride I feel that I've been able to kick a bad habit. My skin doesn't break out the way it used to, my stomach rarely hurts. Friends and family notice a difference in me.

Can you tell from this first draft that she is feeling defeated about her ability to create a new habit? Words like "finally" and phrases like "free of stress eating" and "no longer feel" are good hints. "I don't wake up feeling angry at myself ..." says that she is currently waking up feeling guilty. This isn't a very empowering designed future. Can you tell? Let's look at how she rewrote her second draft:

Designed Future, Second Draft

My body is healthy and balanced. I love my new relationship with food, my eating habits, and myself. I take care of my body, feeding it the nourishment it craves throughout the day. Food is fuel, and the healthier I feed my body, the better it runs. My clear skin is a reflection of this. I remember having had stomachaches at one point and I am grateful to have figured out how to stop them. I am proud of myself for my accomplishment in creating a new habit and love how people in my life have noticed that I look very healthy. Most of all though, I love how my body moves with ease throughout that day.

Step Two
Take Massive Action

Making big changes requires massive action. And with massive action, you need to be willing to fail again and again, and not stop taking action until you get the result you want.

This is how I have built my business. This has been a twenty-plus-year journey of massive action and massive failures. But if my IC had been in control of my mind along this journey, I would not be where I am today. She would have made me quit a long time ago.

Because I am constantly managing my mind and unhooking from my IC's grip, all of my failures have taught me what not to do and helped me figure out the next action to take. I pivot and change, regroup and rework. Over and over and over. I don't let my IC get in the way of my higher commitment. I let her scream, and I take her with me as I continue my journey.

She likes to keep her focus on the failures, setbacks, and possible dangers that lie ahead. I like to keep my eye on the future I am creating. I pay attention to how far I've come and what I've created so far. And that truly blows my mind. I generate excitement because I am so proud of my accomplishments, and know there's so much more ahead to create.

When I hit a pitfall or an obstacle, I let that guide me along my journey. Sometimes I have had to go right back to the drawing board and try again. But my vision for creating massive shifts in the way people think and live their lives all by mastering their minds is what compels me to stay in action no matter what. I have fallen down many times. But that is always what happens when you are in massive action. Failure is just part of the process.

The key to taking massive action is being willing to feel all the discomfort that brings. To feel discomfort, on purpose, over and over again. To learn that you can overcome anything. To never stop, and to continue to manage your mind when your IC is screaming the loudest.

When you are creating your future, whether it is in the realm of your health, business, or relationships, ask yourself, "In the face of my future vision, am I willing to fail as many times as it takes?" If the answer is yes, then you are ready to take massive action.

Most people don't take massive action because they don't know that they are separate from the voice of their IC. So when their IC starts talking, they quit. They give up and say, "This isn't working."

But you know that you don't have to listen to your IC when she's screaming at you. You know that if you have the urge to stop taking action, it's because your IC is trying to prevent you from feeling an emotion. Shame, inadequacy, embarrassment, failure, rejection, these are all feelings that your IC's habitual thoughts will create.

If you are willing to feel those emotions and use them to learn and grow and figure out what's next, this is how you stay on the journey. Because you know that the worst that can happen is that you get uncomfortable. But not taking action is just as uncomfortable – and often even more so. Because at least when you are uncomfortable but taking action, you are in the process of designing your future. It is exhausting and emotionally draining to know that you want something different, and to do nothing about it. Inaction literally sucks the life out of people.

Massive action does come with its own discomfort and exhaustion. But it also comes with exhilaration, aliveness, vitality, and pure joy.

Step Three
Access Your Authentic Self

Pay attention to what you will focus on, then steer your life in the direction of your focus. If, in the past, you automatically focused on what was missing rather than what you already had, you likely found it impossible to feel happy. After all, what you focus on determines how you feel. My suggestion is that you make it a daily practice to put your focus on gratitude. The more you know you are blessed, the more your energy changes. You can't experience anger and gratitude simultaneously. You can't experience fear and gratitude simultaneously.

Gratitude comes naturally to the Authentic Self. And when your Authentic Self has conscious control of your thoughts, you have access to a new part of your mind. A part that is already at peace. A part that is not dependent on other people or any goals in order to feel good. What emerges is a different self. A new and improved self that is redirecting your mind, because you are practicing unhooking from your IC.

When an event or person triggers you back into the clutches of your Inner Critic, you can simply shift into that new mind, right in the moment when you catch your IC engaging in her small, limited, fearful thoughts. The voice of your AS will become louder and louder until it predominates. The more you catch yourself in the limited beliefs and fears of your IC, you can interrupt its old programming of your Inner Critic.

It is a process of unlearning. Instead of blindly following your IC's mind chatter, you are gaining conscious control and interrupting the knee-jerk IC reaction created by some circumstance or person. Waking up to your IC is part of creating a new self and a new life. You are breaking the addiction to the habitual emotional reaction your Inner Critic has been whipping up for forever.

Step Four
Rewrite Your Past from the Perspective of Your Authentic Self

The more time you spend ruminating over your past, the more your past will determine your future.

Your IC assigns a lot of meaning to the circumstances of your past. But if you continue to believe all the lies she's told you about what happened, you will continue to literally recreate that past. That's by design. Since her intention is to keep you safe from her perceived threats, she actively thwarts your growth by keeping you from taking massive action and moving forward.

Your brain is filled with records of the past that were actually written by your IC. But when your Authentic Self is in charge, you're able to look not to the past but toward the future you are designing. You can see what's possible. That means letting go of all that has happened up until this very moment. Successful people need to be willing to sacrifice the mind they have been using for a different mind.

Your Inner Critic thinking is what has given you your current life. Her thoughts are old, familiar, and repetitive. And because of this, her thoughts are in some way comfortable. You don't have to do any conscious work to change them. Your mind can just stay asleep. Designing a new life, on the other hand, can get very uncomfortable – because you have to wake up.

Letting the habitual thoughts go will cause your IC to scream from fear. Your IC only likes predictability and control; she doesn't like to sit in the unknown. Of course, when we are creating a new life, we have to sit in the unknown – and stay in the unknown. This is the paradox of life. The more we want predictability and control, the more we suffer. But when we can train ourselves to sit in the discomfort over and over again, life becomes exciting. The discomfort is deliberate and on purpose. You have to delay the gratification and not get caught up in the current evidence. Don't define yourself by your current results. Give up being a victim and stop struggling.

You have to give up whoever or whatever it is you're blaming for your past and current circumstances. Keep your thoughts, feelings, and actions on the results you want, not the results you have. Examine your thoughts that have created your current life and ask yourself, "Am I willing to let those thoughts go?"

Designing the life you want means taking full responsibility for your thoughts and the actions created by them – and that means creating different thoughts and actions than the ones that got you to where you are now. You can't change the world and then change yourself. You have to change yourself first.

This is where your Authentic Self comes in. Your current life is a reflection of what your Inner Critic has been telling you and what you've believed were your own beliefs. When you access your Authentic Self, you are getting to the mind that lies underneath your IC mind. By continually unhooking from your IC thoughts, you train your mind into new beliefs that serve the life you want to create.

Your new mind, the one where your Authentic Self is in charge, is the roadmap you want to create. Not the map created by your IC, who tells you how hard things have been and how painful things are going to be. Allow your AS to guide you in thinking about your goal as if it's already here, taking the actions consistent with that goal, and then doing it over and over again.

Step Five
Observe Your Inner Critic in Survival Mode

Remember that your IC is designed around fear, which, from an evolutionary standpoint, keeps humans alive. Remember that old commercial trying to illustrate the effects of drug abuse by cracking an egg into a hot frying pan and the announcer saying, "This is your brain on drugs"? Similarly, when your IC speaks, this is just your brain on fear. Your IC's reactions are actually built into your DNA to help you survive. But when you use the part of your brain that is connected to fear, you're using a part that's incapable of reason, creativity, and compassion. Instead, you're using a part that's a reactive, reflexive machine, pre-programmed since birth to prioritize perceived safety over joy.

Your IC mind is basically incapable of rational thought. Worse, your IC actually prevents you from accessing the part of your brain that *is!* And because your brain doesn't know the difference between a real threat and a perceived threat, you're often using your IC mind to try to predict and control your future. This is sheer, instinctive survival – the direct opposite of designing your life from the future.

When you design your life from the future, you connect to something greater than yourself. You know that wherever life will take you, you will be able to handle it. You can cultivate a state of gratitude because you feel that the future you're designing has already happened. Because you trust in a future that you can't see, you can relax into the present and no longer live in survival-based fear mode.

The old thoughts and feelings from your IC are now liberated because you know that those thoughts and feelings are nothing more than old habits of thinking. When you stop thinking from your habitual IC mind, you interrupt what you have taken for granted for your whole life as "normal." As the old thinking gets dismantled, the memories to which your IC assigned her automatic meaning will also be dismantled. Your memories will now not hold the same emotional charge as they once did. You will be able to look back on these memories, and recognize the life lessons that these memories provided, and the wisdom you gained in having those experiences.

When you practice Dethroning Your Inner Critic on a daily basis, you will be able to look back on who you were when your IC was in charge of your mind, and it will seem like another lifetime ago. When you access a new part of your mind, you have the power to reinvent and design a new life.

The unknown and unpredictability of life is what drives your IC mind crazy. She doesn't know what's going to happen, how it's going to go, how you're going to feel, which direction life is going to take. And she *hates* it! She wants to stay comfortable, which is all about predictability. That is the survival mode.

But possibility actually lives outside your comfort zone. Accessing your Authentic Self can change the lens through which you experience and embrace change.

Step Six
Embrace Life Outside Your Comfort Zone
Most people never fulfill their dreams because they're unaware of their IC's deeper commitment: keeping them inside their comfort zone. This is why most people live, *at best,* a "fine" life when they are ruled by their ICs. In their relationships with themselves, their careers, their life partner, their children – nothing is great, but it's "fine." Normal life, for them, means that the limited feelings inside the comfort zone are as good as it's going to get. Moments of bliss are few and far between.

The ongoing work of Dethroning Your Inner Critic, however, is about living an entire life of bliss. And that means continually pushing yourself outside your comfort zone. As you move closer to the edge of your comfort zone, where everything is no longer balanced and "normal," you will feel the survival mechanism of your IC hard at work trying to preserve the status quo. The edge of the comfort zone is the edge of the unknown and the unfamiliar. She's going to resist.

Major transitions, like becoming a mother, or getting a divorce, changing careers, or having a child who is struggling emotionally, will bring you completely outside of what is familiar and predictable. But if you look back on those times in your life where you were in transition or change, you might be able to see how it went: it started out as predictable and normal, then went to off-center, then onto the edge of the unknown, then out into the complete unknown, and then back to normal.

Can you think of examples in your own life? I have a client who lost her entire life savings because her then-husband embezzled all of their finances in a Ponzi scheme. Talk about needing to embrace life outside of your comfort zone! She had to be willing, with a lot of support, to sit in the discomfort of the unknown for many years and continue to take actions that were in alignment with her new life. She had to repeatedly unhook from her IC thoughts and feelings, and act from the new future she was designing.

Today, she's living a new life with a new husband. Although her ex-husband served jail time, she was even able to find forgiveness and remains friends with him to this day. This is all because she created a new relationship with the unknown and what was possible for her moving forward. She repeatedly got her IC out of power, all day, every day, moment by moment as she was designing her future. She embraced discomfort and uncertainty step by step as she reinvented a whole new life.

How is it to look at your life in this way? What is preventing you from staying in the unknown?

Consider what it is that you're really protecting yourself from, and the cost of that protection. Your life gets smaller and smaller when you avoid change and risk, because you're trying to fit life into the parameters of your comfort zone. We create so many obstacles because we want to stay under the illusion of safety! It's an illusion, though, that we can actually predict and control where life goes, one we buy into so we can feel the false sense of safety that creates.

Is safety and security *really* what you're going for?

Step Seven
Design Your Life Questions

Answering these questions helps you access the part of your mind that lies below your IC thoughts:

- What have I achieved in my life?
- When in my life was I most joyful?
- When were things most challenging?
- How did I overcome my most challenging moments, and what did I learn from them?
- What made me feel most proud?
- What have I found most rewarding?
- What challenges, mistakes, or failures actually became opportunities that changed my life?
- What values did I try to remain true to in my life? What helped me remain true to those values?
- What got in the way of my remaining true to those values?
- What life goals have I accomplished so far?
- What motivated me to create those goals?
- Who has had the greatest impact on my life so far?
- With whom do I want to share my gratitude?
- With whom do I have emotional issues that I want to resolve?
- Which of my current habits do I want to keep and develop?
- Which of my habits do I want to eliminate?
- What things have I really wanted to do but failed to do?
- What were the reasons that I couldn't do the things I wanted to do?
- How would I be creating balance effortlessly?
- Where would I be expressing joy and love?
- How would I be accessing my personal power?

- How would I be supporting myself to be in action?
- How would I be practicing self-acceptance?
- How would I be generating my vitality?
- Where would I be reinventing myself?
- What would my relationship to the unknown be?
- How would I be being in my relationships?

Take your time with these questions. Giving up an old identity and stretching for a new one is about investigating how your Inner Critic has been conditioned to protect that old identity. To successfully navigate real change, you have to hear a different calling, something that calls you forth into new ways of being and new actions.

The larger your calling, the more your Inner Critic will scream. And her screams create a lot of discomfort. This is all a normal part of your growth and transformation. Allow yourself to practice discomfort on purpose. Remember, uncomfortable emotions and feelings are nothing more than vibrations in your body. And even more, the physical sensations of fear and excitement are exactly the same. Your heart beats fast, your breathing gets shallow, your hands get clammy. The only difference is the thoughts in your mind.

As you are designing your new future, see yourself living your life from what's possible rather than what you are afraid of. When you practice living from possibility, you start to see and relate to your life differently. You can actually generate the feeling of excitement just by changing your thoughts from fear of "what if" to excitement about what's possible.

Again, remember that the whole spectrum of feelings you feel when declaring your future is normal. This is no small task. You are in the beginning stages of designing a new you. The fear is normal. But so is excitement.

Step Eight
Visualize the Steps

Visualizing yourself doing the steps it takes to reach your vision makes you more likely to succeed. Interestingly, research shows that people who visualized themselves studying get better scores than those who simply just visualized getting a positive grade.

You can apply this research to your own visualization and goals for the future.

Visualization is a woefully underutilized technique, but it's always available to you. Visualization can't, of course, guarantee results in your life. Life *has* no guarantees, unfortunately, and success is a combination of hard work, grit, and even luck. But the more you stay the course, the more likely you are to propel yourself further down the line and learn a hell of a lot about yourself in the process.

So let's have some straight talk about visualization. Visualization doesn't come easily for everyone – like anything, it takes practice. To start you in your visualization process, here are some adapted questions from Mel Robbins for you to ask yourself and consider. Each question is designed to support you in the visualization process to get you to where you want to be. For the purposes of this exercise imagine first that it's five years from now, and you are living your ideal life, and then do the same for one year out from now.

Five years from now:

1. How do you respond when you first meet someone and are asked, "What do you do?"
2. Describe your physical surroundings in as much detail as possible. Where do you live? Where do you spend your free time? Where are you working?
3. Describe the people surrounding you in your personal life (and professional life if applicable).
4. What is the atmosphere in your personal life? Your home life? Your professional life? How do you contribute to those atmospheres?
5. What are you most proud of?
6. What is your favorite way to spend your downtime?

7. When somebody asks you for mentoring advice, what do you tell them?
8. Describe the steps you had to take to get to where you are.
9. Do you have any regrets? Explain.
10. What would you have done differently to get here?

Now, go back and run through these questions as if it's one year from now.

Once you answer the questions and have your vision, write down or think about the steps that you'll need to take to get there. What exactly will you need to do? For the next thirty days, practice visualizing those steps by visualizing both your future vision and the steps you need to take to get there.

Step Nine
Daily Meditation

Meditation has been practiced for centuries. When you meditate every day, you consciously, deliberately, and intentionally make space to see your IC's old, habitual thinking. This is the only way to break the addiction to taking guidance from her.

You have been living with your IC's voice as the guiding force of your life for as long as you can remember. It's time to take back the keys to the kingdom of your mind and reassert dominion. This takes conscious attention on a daily basis.

Meditation is an important tool for disallowing the old beliefs, attitudes, memories, and perceptions to run your mind. The moment you have an "old brain" thought or feeling, you will be able recognize it as your IC's old programming and unhook from it. Instead of identifying yourself with your IC mind, which is who you've always known yourself to be, you begin the work of reprogramming your mind by unlearning your old pattern of thinking and rewiring a new mind with new patterns of thinking.

If you've never meditated much before, love meditating to sounds or music, or could use some guidance, you'll find lots of great meditation tools, recordings, and apps online. Take a look at Inside Timer, Calm, and guided meditations on YouTube, like those from John Kabat-Zinn.

This is how you change who you are, by accessing who you really are underneath your IC mind. And when you change who you are, you change every aspect of your life.

Step Ten
The "I Am" Statement

"I am" are words that will allow you to design your life using a new mind.

Those two words recently literally saved my dad's life. My dad has been battling pancreatic cancer since 2015. It was caught early and treated surgically and successfully the year before my parents retired to Florida. But soon after they began their new life, the doctors discovered two new lesions on his pancreas during a routine check-up.

I had already taught my dad how to use visualization to imagine his future life. And so my dad, now seventy-five, decided that even though his cancer had returned, his life was going to be filled with joy, fun, and peace. Every morning he meditated on this and, in his mind, said, "**I am** living a healthy, vibrant life filled with love and connection."

My parents have seriously not stopped. They've made new friends and actually have a busier social life than I do. But here's the best part. As I was writing this book, my dad received the results from his latest CAT scan. Here's the text I got from my mom:

"Miracle city! Cat scan showed NO evidence of metastatic cancer at all. That means BOTH LESIONS have disappeared!!!!"

My mom told me that when they got the news, she started crying. She turned to my dad and said, "Larry, can you believe it?"

My dad, in his stoic way, said, "Yes, I can. I've been envisioning that the lesions are shrinking and that I am living a healthy and vibrant life."

My dad is still going to stick to his chemo regimen, but this is the best thing ever in my life. And it illustrates the power of our thoughts and beliefs more than anything else I've experienced.

Changing your life begins with aligning your thoughts, feelings, and actions with your future. You have to be willing to actually *become* someone else – the you that you will be. You need to visualize it ahead of time, actually drum up the emotions ahead of time. Not "I will be," but **"I am."**

What does it feel like to see yourself living the life of a confident person? What does it feel like to already have that successful career? What does it feel like to be a healthy person?

When I was a teenager, I struggled with my weight. My grandmother, who was in her eighties at the time, was swimming laps every day and playing doubles tennis. So at the age of fifteen, I decided that I wanted to be like my grandmother. I wanted to be someone who was able to do what she did at eighty. And that is who I became.

I have never struggled with weight again, because who **I am** is someone who takes care of my body. I don't need to have willpower or strength. I take care of my body because of the way it makes me feel to have a healthy body. So if I'm starving, I won't go for the donut in front of me because a donut doesn't occur as a choice. It just isn't an option, because who **I am** is someone who has a healthy body. And if I do eat something like a good dessert, which I love, it is because I'm making a conscious decision to choose that food because I am treating myself.

There's a lot of fear around changing your life because you have to risk feeling uncomfortable emotions. But the fear of feeling the uncomfortable emotions is worse than the actual experience of the uncomfortable emotions.

Remember me standing on the dinner plate–sized platform, afraid to step off? I decided then that I would rather feel afraid on purpose. Because **I am** a confident and courageous woman, and I don't let fear stop me.

If you're standing on a metaphorical cliff and you're afraid to step off, don't wait until you hit a wall. Until you can't stand your life anymore because you have run away from discomfort for so long. I want you to be your own best support. To trust yourself enough to be willing to fail, or feel embarrassed, or get rejected, and to know that you can handle the emotion that goes with that. Because the only thing that the uncomfortable emotion brings up is a feeling. That's it. And you can feel it, and get right back up and keep taking the actions that support the life you are creating.

You have to learn to train your mind to be stronger than your old thoughts, feelings, and emotions, or else you'll lose yourself every time. My suggestion is to write down an **I am** statement. Just pick one from your life. Write it down and post it to your bathroom mirror, your closet door, your desk at work, your dashboard of your car. Visit this statement every day. Visualize what it feels like to already be that.

Step Eleven
Redefine Problems as Opportunities

Everything that happens in your life brings you a choice: get sucked into your IC's drama and dig into your fear, doubt, insecurity, and lack of confidence; or practice separating yourself from her.

The latter might feel scary. Your IC's voice has been with you for so long that it may be the only identity you've ever known. Choosing to ignore her criticism is bound to create change. And if you fear change, you may resist freeing yourself from your IC, and that resistance will give her the control she craves to run your life.

Your IC wants you to believe that you can protect yourself from the very things that frighten you the most – and that you can do so by fixing or changing some part of yourself. In order to get your attention, she catastrophizes – everything that has happened, is happening, or will happen is something horrible that needs your immediate attention and action.

But life, remember, only goes your way about half the time. The other half, things happen. Breakdowns occur. You can never rid yourself of problems – they will be part of your life forever. But what you can do is frame them differently. Your problems actually serve you. They have a purpose.

Your willingness to take a new look at problems as opportunities, rather than things that have gone "wrong," will take some of the anger, frustration, and upset out of the equation. A problem is always a lesson that can teach us something so that we can continue to grow.

I have learned more about myself and my life commitments through the problems and challenges I have faced than I have through my successes and triumphs. I don't regret any of my failures or mistakes because they propelled me to where I am now.

Our problems help us experience who we *don't* want to be and what we *don't* want. And so it is our problems that point us toward who we want to be and the lives we want to live. Problems have the ability to push us outside our comfort zone. If we live life trying to avoid problems, we are more committed to staying safe than to experiencing opportunity and joy. If we never step outside our comfort zone, we stay small.

Step Twelve
Make Friends with Fear

Your IC is bent on trying to manipulate you and your life so that you never have to feel pain. To do so, she whips up your fear of ever experiencing pain. But fear, like happiness, sadness, and anger, is just a feeling. What if you could release the idea that fear is a problem to avoid?

Many of us are so afraid of being afraid that we'll go to great lengths to avoid anything that might inspire fear. But the relentless pursuit of safety means we see our lives as inherently threatening; the more we try to avoid fear by controlling that which we have no control over, the more out of control we feel – and so we try to control more of our experience than ever by seeking self-protection in shutting down. Life becomes a constant struggle of trying to keep our sense of fear, insecurity, and weakness from being triggered.

But fear, like all feelings, is temporary. It passes, and it passes all the more quickly when you stop stuffing it down and fighting it. Trying to control the world so that no one and nothing can cause you discomfort is like standing on a street corner with a box fan and trying to control the direction of the wind. It's exhausting and it's pointless.

Instead, practice noticing when you are feeling afraid, and allowing the feeling to exist. Observe it. Feel it. And in doing so, let it build, crescendo, and pass through you. Fear passes. You can ride it out.

Until now, you, like most of us, have allowed your Inner Critic to decide how things should be. But how things "should be," according to your IC, is a moving target, because your life – and you – will never satisfy her. Instead, she dangles the prospect of you never making mistakes, never feeling afraid, never experiencing pain, never rocking the boat, and never challenging the status quo like a carrot on a stick. It's a fantasy, but when you fall for it, you end up spending your life trying in vain to make that fantasy a reality.

Your IC tricks you into believing that your life will be magically better at some point in the future. But your life only occurs right now. It's not later when you change the career, lose the weight, find the relationship, move to the new house, or retire. Your life will always be right now. So you may as well learn to think thoughts that have you enjoy your life right now, because it's not going to get any better than right now, until you learn to feel better about your life right now.

You, not your Inner Critic, are the designer of your life. You get to decide what things look and feel like, what colors to splash around. Stop painting by number, and start finger-painting instead. It's your life to make of what you will.

CHAPTER EIGHT

DETHRONING YOUR INNER CRITIC IN DAILY LIFE

You can't let fear paralyze you. The worse that can happen is you fail, but guess what: You get up and try again. Feel that pain, get over it, get up, dust yourself off, and keep it moving.

QUEEN LATIFAH

Now that you know exactly what the M.I.N.D Method is all about, it's time to understand what this looks like in your everyday life. Remember, the M.I.N.D. Method is a *moment-by-moment* practice. It is developing the muscle to catch your habitual, conditioned IC thoughts in the midst of her whipping up drama. That shift can only occur when you maintain ongoing awareness.

When you are intimately familiar with the thoughts generated from your IC (M Step), the Indication Signs that those thoughts have invaded your mind (I Step), and the Never-ending Message that those thoughts trigger (N Step), you can recognize when your IC is on her throne right away. When you see clearly see her, you can loosen her grip on you and shift into your new mind to design your life (D Step).

That's the practice. It's simple, but far from easy. Because maintaining conscious awareness is an ongoing, everyday effort, there will be times you slip or forget or go unconscious and get sucked back into your IC mind. After all, she has been running your life for almost as long as you can remember. It's okay. When you notice, simply bring yourself back to center.

Remember that when you use the DYIC tools, there is no such thing as an arrival point, a place you reach where you're all done. This is a practice to use for the rest of your life. But the more you practice, the easier it gets. More importantly, the more you practice, the more you detox yourself from your IC's demands. This frees you to live a life in which you have a deeper sense of well-being and peace of mind, along with the ability to remain in love and connection with yourself and with other people.

Your Inner Critic is an addict, and, like any addict, uses your "drug" of choice in order to keep you seeking pleasure or avoiding pain. Your IC has addictions to being valued, important, loved, making sure you're not judged, and making sure no one is upset with you. This is because your IC's primary addiction is making sure you are *enough* of something – smart enough, pretty enough, good enough, rich enough, young enough. She is addicted to what she sees are your problems.

Your IC's addictions and demands – her very existence - disrupts many areas of your life, threatening your very happiness. But her presence is perhaps most surprising when you realize she's in your relationships too.

This can be the most jarring as you begin to achieve awareness of and some discernment about the voice of your IC – but others around you have not done the same work themselves. Not everyone will be thrilled by your new insights or the changes you may make as a result. In fact, most humans regard change as a threat. It's that primitive, fear-based part of the brain at work, believing that keeping everything and everyone in stasis is critical to survival.

Even positive change – you stop judging and nagging your kids, you cease micromanaging your partner's responsibilities and making yourself responsible for their happiness, you no longer

anxiously check in with your boss on every step of every project –
can be perceived as unwelcome, simply because it's different from
what others have come to expect from you.

It may help to remember that you aren't the only one with
an IC nattering in your head. Your partner, your friends, your
family, your kids, your boss – literally everyone you meet is also
living with an Inner Critic who rules their mind just as surely as
your IC does you. And every one of these Inner Critics is fearful
and fully invested in being "right."

The good news is that you can apply the M.I.N.D. Method
steps to your relationships with others just as surely as you can
to your relationship with yourself. You **Meet Your Inner Critic**
when you recognize her voice in the thoughts you're having
about another person ("My daughter acts like such a baby about
cleaning her room," or "My husband should exercise more.").
You **Identify the Indication Signs** when you acknowledge how
those thoughts make you feel: angry, frustrated, fearful, tightness
in your chest. You **Neutralize the Never-Ending Message** ("I'm
not a good enough mother," or "My value is in taking care of
others."). You choose consciously to shift out of your IC mind and
into your new mind, one that will allow you to **Design Your Life**
with your husband and daughter so that you can remain loving
and connected even when you are upset.

Like DYIC itself, this will take practice. Even when you learn
how to get your Inner Critic out of your relationships, you will
still have moments when you find yourself trying to fix, change,
and control others and calling it love.

The important thing to remember here is that love is not a
concept or a thing. It's an action verb. It's a way of being. Your
relationships, therefore, are also not things. They are made up,
instead, of a series of actions that *you* take, and those actions need
to be consistent with the kind of relationship you want to create.
If you want a peaceful, loving relationship, notice whether your
way of being in that relationship will produce that.

Remember that when it comes to your relationships, just as
anywhere else in your life, someone is always in charge of your

actions. Do you want that someone to be your Inner Critic, operating from fear, or you, choosing to generate a different way of being? When you develop the ability to remain loving even in the face of upsets, you're on the road to creating extraordinary relationships.

As you practice DYIC, be on the lookout for backslides into old thoughts, which lead to old behaviors. You may find yourself once again worrying about what you did (or didn't) do that meant you didn't get that thing or outcome you wanted. You may catch yourself obsessing about whether or not people actually like you. You may consciously or unconsciously still find yourself focusing on what you can do to feel safe.

Your brain is like a huge biocomputer – a complex piece of machinery. This book has given you the owner's manual, but a manual can't help if you don't read and adhere to it. That would be like getting into a car every day and not knowing how to drive it. You may indeed move the car, but you won't get very far before crashing into something and causing a lot of pain and damage.

Effectively using your biocomputer means consciously and repeatedly giving yourself instructions that interrupt the old programming created by your IC's fear-based addictions and demands. Your Inner Critic believes that life is made up of near-constant danger and directs you to avoid risk. Even when you take action and actually get what you want, your IC flips from fear to addiction to next solution to the next thing she sees as a problem. Now she just wants more and more solutions to the same problem – that you aren't enough of something.

That's why we can continue to feel unhappy and unfulfilled no matter how many goals or accomplishments we achieve. Our IC is always focused on the next addiction. As you continue to practice Dethroning Your Inner Critic, the more you will clearly see your addictive programming, and learn to repeatedly catch it and detach from it. You stop allowing your IC to keep you stuck in your addictions to your problems. Instead, your newly rewired mind becomes committed to a life of freedom, joy, and inner peace.

Mary, the vice president of a large pharmaceutical company, participated in one of my Mastering Your M.I.N.D. programs. She was struggling with what she felt was her CEO's constant criticism, which left her feeling tense, angry, and exhausted not only at work, but at home with her husband and kids.

When Mary began to practice the M.I.N.D. Method, she realized how much of her life she'd spent listening to Queen Inadequate and Queen Perfectionist, trying to ward off the judgment of others. A superstar student in school and a people-pleaser from a young age, she'd flourished personally and professionally. She began to see, though, that her IC's addition to nonstop praise and success meant she was devastated by the threat of anyone who criticized her.

She clearly saw that this addiction has its roots in her childhood. She and her siblings were often criticized by her father, whose own parents had made him feel worthless and so had spent his life overcompensating to heal his wounded self-esteem. Blind to his own Inner Critic's addiction to overachievement and perfectionism, he'd come to believe that "good" parenting meant pointing out every instance in which his kids could have done or been better. Recognize Queen Perfectionist at work?

Accordingly, Mary's biocomputer kicked into overdrive whenever she felt like her dad was disappointed in her. She recalled an incident at age six, when her dad told her she wasn't playing her best in a peewee basketball game. Mary felt both ashamed and less than, like she'd been punched in the gut. Years later, she could still remember where she was standing on the basketball court when her dad expressed his disapproval. This is because when our brain senses danger, it hones in on all the details: the smell in the room, where we are standing, who was around us. Remembering what felt like threats to our survival is our brain's job.

But now Mary was a grown, powerful, accomplished woman with a family of her own. She had to practice the intense discomfort of potentially being criticized. Instead of trying to censor her opinions to ward off criticism, and then feeling resentful and powerless, Mary practiced aligning her behavior with the life she was designing. Instead of being driven by her IC's default commitment to prevent criticism, Mary stepped into her new mind, which was committed to being a confident, powerful leader in her industry and in her life. She felt the discomfort, but found her voice again and again.

As she kept practicing new behaviors that were aligned with designing her new life, she learned that she could handle it if another person criticized or judged her. She downgraded her IC addiction to a preference. Of course she would prefer not to be criticized or judged, but she no longer saw judgment as a problem that needed to be prevented. Mary learned to unhook from the need to control other people's judgment. She realized that she could deliberately have thoughts that allowed her to recognize the unbelievable accomplishments she has had in her life, and how loved she is by her friends and family.

She started to learn how to think in a way that had her fall in love with herself, so she didn't *need* other people's approval in order to feel good. Her feelings of happiness were no longer connected to anything that was occurring outside of HER. She was able to step back and witness all the drama that her IC created, from an inner place of calm and peace within. And this is because she shifted into a newly relocated part of her mind. Not her old, everyday mind that she had identified with for most of her life, and used to look through.

Mary created a completely new relationship with herself, one in which she no longer doubted and second-guessed herself. Because she felt calm inside, she began interacting with her husband and kids in a different way.

This is the beautiful thing that starts to happen when you practice the M.I.N.D. Method. You just don't get as triggered by other people. You realize that their behavior is about their automatic IC thoughts that create their automatic emotions that lead to their automatic behaviors. You understand on a deep soul level that their behavior is about them, and you interrupt your IC's attempts to make it about you.

You have more room for people's jerkiness. Because people will act like jerks – even the ones that we love. But when we don't take their jerkiness personally, we stop being so reactive to everyone and every circumstance around us. We can just be. We stop feeling like other people are scary. We no longer need to protect ourselves from their judgments or rejections.

As you continue to practice using your biocomputer effectively, you can continue to catch your IC mind whipping up drama, unhook from that old mind, and step in a new mind. It's very much like exercise. If you want a fit body, you have to exercise daily. If you want a new, calmer, mind, you have to practice daily.

When you upgrade your thoughts to match your newly rewired mind, you can fully experience the joy and wonder of your current wild and precious life. It's a gentle shift, not a forceful one. It is a subtle glimpse of letting go. Shifting away from your IC demands, and shifting into allowing other people to have whatever opinions or judgments they are going to have.

You will always have the opportunity to practice this, just as I did a few weeks ago with my father. Now, I love my dad dearly, but he has a lot of opinions and judgments. Anyone else you know have a father like that? It's a challenge because my Inner Critic's demand, formed in my childhood, is wanting everyone to like me, value me, and think well of me. I'm not alone here. This is probably *the* most common demand from most people's Inner Critic.

I was on vacation with my family and my parents, and we were swimming in a beautiful lake together. All of a sudden, my dad's mood took a turn and he became judgmental and critical about how I handled a situation with my twelve-year-old daughter. But instead of going down the rabbit hole of anger, defensiveness, blame, resentment, and then trying to convince him that his judgment of me was wrong, I just listened.

I didn't allow his judgment to rob me of my inner peace. I allowed him to have his judgment, and I didn't let my Inner Critic's demand that he not judge me knock me off center. In other words, I accepted the fact that he had his judgment. I didn't try to change it or prove him wrong. I let it be. And I stayed connected to my love for him, in spite of his judgment.

I said to him, "Dad, I hear that you think I should have handled it differently. I hear that you think my daughter should have handled herself differently. And this is who I am, and this is who she is. You can either continue to be upset or you can enjoy this beautiful lake and this beautiful day. And I love you."

And I swam away. It became his choice to either stay in his anger and frustration, or to enjoy the moment. Either way, I wasn't knocked out of my peace.

Because I didn't react with anger, like my Inner Critic would have had me do in the past, I was able to enjoy the moment swimming in the lake. I didn't go down the rabbit hole of Inner Critic thoughts like, "How dare he judge me. He doesn't know the first thing about parenting," and whatever other drama my Inner Critic might have whipped up.

Other people have their experiences. You have yours. You then realize that you are okay no matter what happens, and you can handle all of your emotions. You no longer have to control life so that you only feel the good emotions. You can stop being afraid to feel. You now know that your emotions are nothing to be afraid of, and that they are simply vibrations within your body.

Interrupting the downward spiraling of unhappiness caused by your IC is now at your fingertips. The shift is about redirecting your focus from outside of yourself to within. When you find yourself trying to manage, fix, or control anything or anyone outside of yourself, that is your opportunity to shift the location of your mind and change your inner programming to your new mind thoughts.

Here are some examples of new mind thoughts that you may find especially useful:

- My life is a journey.
- Any problem is an opportunity for me to grow and learn.

- I don't need anyone else to love me, value me, or think well of me in order for me to be okay.
- Parts of my life will be the way I want it to be, and other parts will not. That is the way life goes.
- Another's behavior is not a reflection of my worthiness or my value.
- My emotional discomfort is all serving my growth.
- Feeling fear and taking action anyway is what will make my dreams come true.
- "Should" is the worst word in the English Language. When I am "shoulding" myself, that is my Inner Critic speaking.
- I don't need to avoid, numb, or run from my negative emotions. They are here to serve my growth.
- I am responsible for creating all of my emotions, as they stem from the thoughts I am choosing to think.
- Producing results in my life is a function of how I feel, as my feelings cause my actions.
- What I am feeling right now is a function of my beliefs.
- When I fully experience a feeling that makes me uncomfortable, the discomfort doesn't last very long.
- I am embracing my emotional maturity by taking responsibility for all of my thoughts and feelings.
- I am no longer letting my IC blame anyone else for my feelings.
- I am not able to control anyone but myself.
- I am able to set the proper boundaries in my relationships, rather than trying to fix, change, or control that person.
- When life doesn't go the way I expected it to, I can learn from the experience.
- I am continuing to learn about who I really am as I unhook from my IC mind.
- I don't have to know where life is going. I can use my new mind to take the next right step and then let life go wherever it will go.
- To be my Authentic Self is to be willing to experience *all* of my emotions.

As you continue to practice shifting to your new mind to Design Your Life, you will begin to notice that you can remain more neutral with people and circumstances that you once found incredibly triggering. Other people's opinions of you may not seem so scary. You now know who you really are. You are not who your IC has said you are. You are detoxing from your attachment that others have to know who you are, too.

If others see who you are, wonderful! They are your people. If they don't see who you are, they are not your people. To quote Eleanor Roosevelt, "What other people think of me is none of my business."

This might mean that some people and relationships, particularly those on the fringes of your life, fall away. This can be disconcerting, but it can also be okay. The newfound inner resources you'll discover will more than make up for the loss of acquaintances who were likely never in your corner to begin with.

As you are looking at designing your life, you may find yourself feeling confused or unsure. You might have thoughts like, "I don't know whether I should stay at my job or find a new one," or, "I don't know whether I should stay in my marriage or leave my marriage," or "I don't know what I want my life to be." When you stay stuck in confusion, here's what's really going on. Your IC is afraid of making the wrong decision. Your IC wants to know how your future is going to go. She wants to predict, control, and script it all. So your IC wants to predict how your future will turn out by figuring out what is the "right" decision so that your life goes exactly the way that you want it to go. And your IC wants life to go a certain way so that you can avoid emotions that will make you feel uncomfortable when you face the unknown.

As you practice designing your life over time, you will see your rewired mind. You will begin to witness yourself handling circumstances differently than you would have in the past. You will start to watch your life unfold in new and exciting ways. Your fear will be overpowered by possibility. You will actually start to look forward to feeling the fear, because you know you can handle that feeling. You can take new actions that will result in creating a whole new life. That is how you design a life you love.

QUESTIONS FOR YOUR CONSIDERATION

- Where are you stuck in confusion or "I don't know" in your life? If you "don't know," remind yourself of what you just learned.
- What feelings come up for you around making decisions? Past decisions, future decisions? Remember that there are no bad decisions, just feelings about decisions. What's the next decision you will make?
- Where is the emotion in your body? Naming your emotion is not enough. Don't just say that you're angry or sad. Find where your emotion is located in your body. Describe the feeling in a way that explains physically what it feels like: Tightness in your chest. A lump in your throat.
- Are there areas where you're feeling great about yourself? Each of us has made a goal happen at some point in our life either consciously or unconsciously. We left that horrible job, we had that child, we found the love of our life, we started that exercise routine, we found that friend. We've all accomplished amazing things in our lives. What's one area of your life that is currently working? How do you know it's working? What qualities can you distinguish about yourself when you think about this area?
- What goals or dreams did you make happen? Can you see one in your mind's eye right now? That particular goal or dream is evidence that you are able to make your goals your reality. You already have a blueprint for success. If you can do it in one area, you can do it in another. Trust yourself to be able to feel whatever it is you're feeling and come out the

other side. Your IC's fear – and, by extension, yours – no longer rules you.

Your mind is going to be with you through thick and thin for the rest of your life. So, if you want your mind to always work with you instead of against you, then you have to learn how to master your mind. You are your own ultimate guide for your journey toward the life you want.

You now know that you can't have the peace, freedom, and joy that you crave by using your old, computer-programmed everyday IC mind. It just doesn't work. You now have the tools to interact with the outside world around you, and work on your inner world, by shifting to your relocated mind. You now have the ability to return to being centered and present no matter what life presents to you. And unlike other conventional methods of growth that require years or decades, using the M.I.N.D. Method to master your mind is about rapidly reprogramming your biocomputer within months. Instead of trying to find your emotional wellbeing by calming your automatic mind, changing your IC thoughts or adjusting your IC's attitudes, you now know that's not possible! Your IC mind has been with you for forever, and it will be with you for forever.

The secret to freedom is using the M.I.N.D. Method to shift into a new mind. You are developing the capacity to see who you really are when you stop listening to your IC and awaken to your full potential as a human being. With the M.I.N.D. Method tools at your disposal, you now have a superpower.

Welcome to your new life. You are a superhero!

CONCLUSION

You find peace not by rearranging the circumstances of your life,
but by realizing who you are at the deepest level.

ECKHART TOLLE

In creating the M.I.N.D. Method and the Dethroning Your Inner
Critic programs, I have worked with women all over the world.
Together, we've created a community of people who are learning
the tools to not only manage their Inner Critic but also create a
new mind, one that allows them to live lives they love and inspires
them to the depths of their core.

Women have struggled, generation after generation, to define
themselves despite being raised with persistent myths of who
we are supposed to be. And since the inception of the feminist
movement in the 1960s, women have been banding together
to eradicate those myths and change our culture. Today, this
feels more urgent and also closer than ever, from the #MeToo
movement to the increasing likelihood of a female president.
Now, more than ever, it is time for women to rise up.

With the Dethroning Your Inner Critic movement, women
now have a possibility to emerge from old habits of thought
and conditioned ways of being, to step into a new level of
empowerment. It is my fervent hope and my life's commitment to
bring this movement to women all over the world.

The M.I.N.D Method allows you to practice Dethroning Your
Inner Critic so you can find and return to your Authentic Self.

It begins by identifying and questioning that delusional IC story that has plagued you for so long. When you hear your Queen Inner Critic for the crank she really is, you'll be able to recast her in a bit part instead of as the lead in your life.

As you make a commitment to practice Dethroning Your Inner Critic every day, you will clearly see that while feeling emotional pain is part of life, the suffering you feel is actually a choice. It's optional.

From this point forward, you can see that the only place your life happens is in the here and now. You can focus on what is happening moment by moment. You are responsible for everything you see in the world and how it all occurs to you. You have that power because it all begins and ends with you. Anything that you are experiencing as a problem is really how you are perceiving it.

By shifting into a new mind, you are able to create a paradigm shift. As you do this work, you will come to see and know that your IC has been trying to fix something that was never broken in the first place. You are already whole and complete. You were born that way. When you practice Dethroning Your Inner Critic, you return yourself to the you that you were before your Inner Critic overpowered your mind.

You're doing something big here. Because most people stay unhappy, waiting for their life to change before they can feel gratitude, abundance, wholeness. That's the old model of cause and effect. They are waiting for something external to create their positive feelings. But you've learned differently. Living from lack doesn't create an abundant and joyful life. Joy is something you generate.

You now know the secret to life: Your thoughts are not facts. They are stories that your Inner Critic made up a long time ago, and that you have simply been relating to as if they were true. Your Inner Critic thoughts are not reality. When you know the difference between you and your Inner Critic, you have won the lottery of life. You can take chances. You can get into what the late

John Lewis called "good trouble." You can be willing to try, even willing to fail. Michael Jordan became "Michael Jordan" because even though he had times when he failed in his life, he didn't think of himself as a failure. He saw failing as an opportunity, a way to grow and get better. He wasn't afraid of failing because he knew it was a part of learning, of mastery, and of becoming a success.

You can see things this way too.

Join us, won't you? The rest of your life is waiting for you.

RESOURCES

BOOKS
- *The Universe Has Your Back,* Gabrielle Bernstein
- *Radical Acceptance,* Tara Brach
- *The Gifts of Imperfection,* Brené Brown
- *Breaking the Habit of Being Yourself,* Dr. Joe Dispenza
- *Untamed,* Glennon Doyle
- *You Say More Than You Think,* Janine Driver with Mariska van Aalst
- *Flex: The Art and Science of Leadership in a Changing World,* Jeffrey Hull, PhD
- *Loving What Is,* Byron Katie and Stephen Mitchell
- *Shift into Freedom,* Loch Kelly
- *Playing Big,* Tara Mohr
- *Big Lessons for Little People,* Lois Nachamie
- *The 5 Second Rule,* Mel Robbins
- *The Four Agreements,* Don Miguel Ruiz
- *The Untethered Soul,* Michael A. Singer
- *Loving Bravely,* Alexandra H. Solomon, PhD
- *A New Earth,* Eckhart Tolle
- *Negotiate Like You M.A.T.T.E.R,* Rebecca Zung, Esq.

PODCASTS
- *Dethroning Your Inner Critic Podcast,* Joanna Fox Kleinman, LCSW
- *The Life Coach School Podcast,* Brooke Castillo
- *UnF*ck Your Brain,* Kara Loewentheil, J.D.
- *The Marie Forleo Podcast,* Marie Forleo
- *On Purpose Podcast,* Jay Shetty
- *The School of Greatness Podcas,* Lewis Howes
- *Impact Theory,* Tom Bilyeu
- *The Ed Mylett Show,* Ed Mylett

ACKNOWLEDGMENTS

I have been fortunate enough to have many people in my life who have contributed to bringing this book to reality. Without their contribution, this book could never have been written.

First, I want to thank my mother, Judy Fox. Your brilliance and wisdom as both my mom and as a psychotherapist are what made this book possible. I am forever grateful to you for the countless hours you have spent collaborating on the ideas that are at the heart of the Dethroning Your Inner Critic work. This book stands on the shoulders of your life's work.

To my father, Larry Fox, I am grateful to you for introducing me to the world of transformational thinking by the age of nine. Your commitment to my emotional and spiritual growth has created a ripple effect that has touched the lives of countless people. Your relentless commitment to sharing your wisdom to all who are blessed to know you is an ongoing gift.

To my husband, Jon, thank you for your infinite support and love, and for calling out my Inner Critic when she is rearing her head. You are my best friend and my rock. Thank you for your unending love.

To my children, Max, Zach, and Amanda, thank you for putting up with all that it took to make this book a reality, and for the ongoing practice that you provide for me to Dethrone my Inner Critic! The three of you are my greatest inspiration.

To my brilliant team from Bloom Admin Services, Nicole Neer and Carrie Hess, thank you for partnering with me to create the business of my dreams.

To my editor Maggie McReynolds, thank you for your amazing talent and all that you contributed to bringing this book to the finish line.

To my friends, your love and friendship has been more important throughout this journey than I can ever express.

To Emily Golden, my former business partner, thank you for your invaluable contribution to my ability to maximize my entrepreneurial spirit.

To Tammi Leader, who gave me the opportunity to lead the first Dethroning Your Inner Critic workshop at Campowerment in 2015, I am forever grateful to you for seeing in me what I couldn't see in myself. You have not only been a champion for me, but for bringing this work to thousands of women.

Many coaches, colleagues, and amazing clients have contributed to this book. Your stories, your willingness to engage with the DYIC distinctions, and your commitment to your own growth have made this book possible. Thank you for your love, your support of my work, and your trust in me to help you rewire your new mind.

ABOUT THE AUTHOR

JOANNA KLEINMAN is a licensed psychotherapist, life and corporate coach, author, podcaster, motivational speaker, and the founder of Dethroning Your Inner Critic. She considers herself to be an unconventional therapist and is driven by the conviction that the most powerful life you can live is when you know the difference between *you* and your Inner Critic.
She developed the M.I.N.D Method, a time-tested, proven system that brings together practical psychology, neuroscience, and the power of intention to discover who you are separate from the critical voice in your mind. With over 25 years' experience, she has worked with corporations such as Campowerment, Cigna, Nestlé, and TD Bank, and has transformed the lives of thousands of people by detailing how they can design a new future through rewiring the automatic way they think and act, and breaking the habit of giving energy and attention to their Inner Critic.

THANK YOU

Thank you for reading this book. I am inspired by your openness to embrace these ideas and apply them to your life. I believe that when you practice the M.I.N.D. Method on a daily basis, you have the owner's manual to master your mind. You have the power to not only transform your own life, but to impact the lives of everyone with whom you cross paths. The ripple effect and the capacity for women to create waves of change that reverberate into their families, their communities, and their businesses is more important than ever.

Whether you want to raise your kids to feel confident and fulfilled, make an impact in your company, or become someone who empowers other women, it all starts with *you!* Women can learn to intentionally think in a way that fosters love, contentment, and peace. We have a chance to change the world. We have a chance to make history – there has never been a greater need for confident women to rise up and be the change we want to see.

Visit my website DethroningYourInnerCritic.com to receive my masterclass videos that help you put the concepts of the M.I.N.D. Method into practice right now. And check out the *Dethroning Your Inner Critic Podcast* on Apple, Stitcher, Soundcloud, or wherever you download your favorite podcasts.

CPSIA information can be obtained
at www.ICGtesting.com
Printed in the USA
LVHW080715090722
723112LV00013B/957